문화부 추천도서 선정
韓國詩大事典

육당 최남선부터 지금까지 (1908년~2023년)

한국詩대사전 개정증보판 발간 안내

　　1985년 한국 최초로 **한국시조큰사전**(한춘섭·박병순·리태극 편저)을 출판한 이래, 여러 시인님들의 적극적인 협조와 격려 덕분에 1988년 **한국시대사전**(구상·정한모·문덕수 감수_김영삼 편저), 2004년 **한국시대사전**(한국時調큰사전과 한국詩대사전을 합본) 개정증보판, 2011년 **한국시대사전**(허영자·윤금초·윤해규 편저)을 발간했습니다.

　　이후 詩사전에 누락된 시인님들의 계속되는 재발간 요청과 성원에 힘을 얻어 처음 발간 이후 39년 만에 다음과 같이 『한국詩대사전』의 개정증보판을 발간하고자 합니다.

을지출판공사 주간 권오운　대표 김효열 드림

＊4×6배판·4,500여 쪽·불변특수지·가죽표지 금박·고급 양장본＊

- 수록 예정 시인 : 4,000여 명
- 대표시(代表詩) : 5편~7편 (150행 이내) ＊편집상 가감될 수도 있습니다.
- 원고 마감일 : 2025년 1월 31일 ＊지면관계상 조기 마감될 수 있습니다.
- 발간 예정일 : 2025년 9월 30일
- 책값(한국詩대사전) : 450,000원 (수록시인에게는 290,000원)

2011년 발행 한국詩대사전

- 4×6배판 3,552쪽
- 수록 시인 : 3,530명
- 수록 시 : 27,380편
- 불변특수지 50g
- 가죽표지 금박 양장본
- 정가 : 290,000원

＊한국詩의 집대성
＊한국詩의 총화
＊한국詩의 정수

을지출판공사
시시전 편집부

04083　서울시 마포구 양화진길 41, 603호(합정동)
Tel. 02-334-4050 · 010-2289-4010　Fax. 02-334-4010
eMail : ejp4010@gmail.com

세계시문학 42집 발간을 축하합니다

내 그림자를 보며

고 방 규

대나무 그림자는
섬돌을 쓸어도
움직이지 않는 티끌
달빛은 호수를 뚫어도
물에는 흔적 하나 없습니다

흘러온 추억에는
이고 짊어질 이야기보따리는
달 수 없는 무게입니다

흙탕물에도
더럽히지 않는 연꽃처럼
주인이 되어 서 있는
내 그림자
지워지지 않습니다

그토록
그리운 그대처럼

The 38th Grand Award of the World Poetry(2024) _ Korea

대상 수상자 : Poet Seo Keun-hee 서근희 시인

* born in Hamyang, South Gyeongsang Province
* graduated from the Department of Food and Nutrition at Sookmyung Women's University
* debuted as a poet in 1989 through the magazine, *The Space of Literature*
* member of the Korean Writers Association
* board member of International PEN/Korean Center
* member of the Korean Female Writers Society
* literary awards : Heo-nan-seol-heon Literary Award, Seongnam Literary Award, Grand Prize of Korean Literature, Grand Prize of Pure Literature, Poet Award of the Korean Modern Poets Association
* collections of her poems: *The Scroll of Time, Picking Up Sunshine, Where Sunshine Stays, I Dish Up Sunshine for You* (vols 1 and 2), *Fragrance of Sunshine*

* 경남 함양 출생
* 숙명여대 식품영양학과 졸업
* 1989년 《문학공간》 신인상 등단
* 한국문인협회 회원
* 국제펜 한국본부 이사
* 한국여성문학인회 회원
* 문학상 : 허난설헌 문학상
　　　　　성남문학상
　　　　　한국문예문학 대상
　　　　　순수문학 대상
　　　　　현대시인협회 시인상
* 시집 : 『시간의 두루마리』
　　　　『햇살 줍기』
　　　　『햇살 고인 자리』
　　　　『햇살 담아드려요 1, 2』
　　　　『햇살의 향기』

제38회 세계시문학 대상(2024) _ 서근희

| Day By Day | 하루하루 |

Living
Is as beautiful as autumn leaves;
is it something to laugh about like flowers?

Deep into the night, it snows in large flakes;
the beautiful snowflakes
flutter down with tears
in the mystery of the universe.

I live in the same way as before,

Trees are not afraid of the night.
Suddenly yesterday the wind blew mischievously;
today the sun is bright, so I'm smiling.
Yes, I live in the same way as before.

If I keep living in the same way as before,
my body shall return to dust.
I'll go to bed with sincere prayer.

사는 것이
가을의 단풍처럼 아름답고
꽃처럼 웃기만 하겠습니까

함박눈 내리는 깊은 밤
우주 속 우주의 신비
스쳐 나온 아름다운 눈송이도
눈물 머금고 내립니다

그냥 그냥 살지요

나무들은 밤이 와도 두려워하지 않습니다
갑작스레 어제는 짓궂게 바람 불더니
오늘은 두터운 햇살이 좋아 웃습니다
그래 그냥 살지요

그냥 그냥 살다 보면
흙으로 돌아가는 몸
벌거벗은 기도 한 자락 깔고 잠드럽니다

The 38th Grand Award of the World Poetry (2024)_ Seo Keun-hee

■ commentary

What Are Poems Going to Do with Our Lives?

All the logic and values of life in the world are as new as its weight and sometimes too much for us to handle, so we are overwhelmed or perceive it as a stepping stone to go further forward. In this way, the logic of life is considered equal before everyone, or only as a dice that has already been thrown.

Therefore, asking, "How can life be as beautiful as autumn leaves and smiling like flowers?" (from her poem 'Day By Day'), poet Seo Keun-hee is not hiding her shame by confessing, "I just live," In that sense, she has an smiling Buddha image carved on a cliff, saying, "Even the mystery of the universe is not an object of fear any more."

I think we can guess her daily life without looking into it. Her poems make us believe she has led her life as it is without pretense.

It is so. What are poems going to do with our lives?

- Judges : Won Eung-soon, Park Young-yul, Gwon O-un

■ 심사평

시가 우리의 삶을 어찌하겠다는 건가

세상의 모든 삶의 이치와 가치는 그것이 지니는 무게만큼 새롭고 때로는 벅차기까지 한 것이어서 이에 우리들은 자지러지기도 하고 앞으로 더 멀리 내닫는 디딤돌로도 인식하거나 한다. 이렇게 볼 때 삶의 이치는 만인 앞에 평등하다거나 이미 던져진 주사위로밖에는 헤아려지지 않기도 한다.

그래서 서근희 같은 시인은 '사는 일이 어찌 가을의 단풍처럼 아름답고 꽃처럼 웃기만 하겠느냐'(시「하루하루」부분)고 반문하면서 '그냥 그냥 살지요'로 자괴를 반추하면서 부끄러움을 감추지 않고 있다. 그러다 보니 '우주의 신비마저도 두려움의 대상이 아니게 되었다'고 외로운 마애불의 웃음 같은 심보를 넌지시 내보이고 있다.

서근희 시인의 일상은 따로 들여다보지 않아도 알 것 같다. 주어진 삶의 무게만큼 포장되지 않은 그대로의 음성만큼만 영위해 가리라는 굳은 신뢰를 꺼내 보여 주었다.

그렇다. 우리 시가 삶을 어찌겠다는 말인가.

－심사위원 : 원응순, 박영률, 권오운(글)

The 38th Main Award of the World Poetry(2024) _ Germany

본상 수상자 : Poet Jhung Anja 정안야 시인

* 8th president of the Korean Writers Society in Germany
* advisory committee member of the Korean Nurses Association in Germany
* debuted as a poet in 2015 through the magazine, *The Literary Trend*
* debuted as an essayist through the magazine, *The Spring of Literature*
* debuted as a novelist through the magazine, *The Literary Trend*
* board member of the Peasant Literature
* member of International PEN/Korean Center
* received the Presidential Citation
* received the Citation from the Korean Consul General in Hamburg
* collection of her poems : *The Eternal House*
* collection of her short stories : *Bells Ringing at Noon*

* 재독 한국문인회 8대 회장 역임
* 재독간호협회 자문위원
* 《문예사조》 시 신인상 등단 (2015년)
* 《문학의 봄》 수필 등단
* 《문예사조》 소설 등단
* 농민문학 이사
* 국제PEN 한국본부 회원
* 대통령 표창장 수상
* 주함부르크 총영사 표창장 수상
* 시집 : 『영원한 그 집』
* 단편소설집 : 『정오의 종소리』

제38회 세계시문학 본상(2024)_정안야

I Will Bloom	**꽃 피우리라**

I walk along the field edge path.

In the green field,
there are many grass flowers in bloom
that have braved snow and rain.

I quietly
carry the flowers
into my mind.

Each grass flower of its own style
is really pretty;
fascinated by their various scents,
I want to get away
from my daily routine.

Even in a world as heavy as a rock,
even in a noisy world,
spring comes after winter;
winter goes again
and spring comes again.

Just like the flowers,
I want to bloom again,
smelling nice.

Like the flowers in that field,
I will bloom.

풀섶 들길을 걷는다

푸르른 저 들판
그동안 눈비 맞으며
소담히 피워 낸 꽃송이 송이들

조용히
내 안에
고이 옮겨 심는다

제멋에 겨운
풀꽃들
오색향기에 취해
얽매였던 낡은 삶을
슬며시 풀어놓고 싶다

바위처럼 무거운 세상
소란스런 세상
겨울 가고 봄 오고
다시 겨울 가고
또 봄이 오듯이

다시 한 번
새순 돋아 보리라
향기롭게 돋게 하리라

저 들판의 꽃들처럼
나도 꽃 피우리라

The 38th Main Award of the World Poetry(2024) _ Jhung Anja

■ commentary

The Difference between Well-Written Poem and Well-Read Poems

It is said there are two types of poems that are 'well-written' and 'well-read'. Strictly speaking, however, well-written poems are well-read poems. People often say, "There are no poetic words." It is not too much to say that we are living in the heyday of so-called "easy poems" these days. Even so, we sometimes come across words that are not poetic and cannot be understood at all. Easy poems mean the works that readers can read and understand without any difficulties.

Poet Jhung Anja's poem attracts our attention as 'a good sample of an easy poem' like this:

I walk along the field edge path// In the green field/ there are many grass flowers in bloom/ that have braved snow and rain// I quietly/ carry the flowers/ into my mind.

There is nothing we cannot understand no matter how much we look at that poem. However, there is no negligence in the meaning or image of the work. I sincerely hope that she will be born again as a poet who can write easy and readable poems.

- Judges: Won Eung-soon, Park Young-yul, Gwon O-un

■ 심사평

잘 쓴 시와 잘 읽히는 시의 차이

흔히 '잘 쓴 시'와 '잘 읽히는 시'가 따로 있다고 한다. 그러나 엄밀히 말하면 '잘 쓴 시'가 곧 '잘 읽히는 시'다. '시어(詩語)가 따로 없다'는 말과 함께 요즘은 이른바 '쉬운 시'의 전성시대에 살고 있다고 해서 그리 지나친 말이 아니다. 그러다 보니 시도 아니고 그 무엇도 아닌 도무지 알아들을 수 없는 소리가 되는 경우도 종종 일어나고 있다. 시가 쉽다는 것은 읽어서 모를 것이 없다는 뜻이다.

시인 정안야의 시는 '쉬운 시의 표본' 같은 작품들이 눈길을 끈다.

'풀섶 들길을 걷는다// 푸르른 저 들판/ 그동안 눈비 맞으며/ 소담히 피워 낸 꽃송이 송이들// 조용히/ 내 안에/ 고이 옮겨 심는다.'

아무리 골똘히 곱씹어 보아도 모를 것이 없다. 그렇다고 의미나 이미지 따위에도 소홀함이 보이지 않는다. 아무쪼록 쉽고 잘 읽히는 시를 쓰는 시인으로 거듭 태어나기를 간절히 바란다.

－심사위원: 원웅순, 박영률, 권오운(글)

The 38th Main Award of the World Poetry(2024) _ Korea

본상 수상자 : Poet Yoon Jeong-in 윤정인 시인

* born in Gangjin, South Jeolla Province
* debuted as a poet through the magazine, The Writing Mountain Range
* received the Grand Award of Poem and Culture
* board member of the Society of World Poetry
* operating director of the poetry group 'Poems Boom' in Gwangju
* CEO of Dasan Organic Rice, 'Clear Embryo Rice'
* collection of his poems : *TThe Way to the House of Dasan*

* 전남 강진 출생
* 《창작산맥》으로 등단
* 포렌컬쳐 최우수상 수상
* 세계시문학회 이사
* 광주《시꽃피다》운영이사
* 다산청정미 '맑은눈의쌀' 대표
* 시집 : 『다산초당 가는 길』

제38회 세계시문학 본상(2024) _ 윤정인

The Way to the House of Dasan

The aroma of tea wafts with the rustle of reed leaves.

The path of the roots is silent.
Counting stone steps, I pass through West Annex.

Under the tall rock where intaglio has been preserved,
a camellia floats in the gourd of Yakcheon Spring.

In front of the old wooden porch, I bow to the portrait.
The taste of hot water for tea gets stuck in my molars.

A duck is sitting on faded fallen leaves;
Yeonji Falls knock on the pedestal rock of Mt. Seokga.

Pink zinnia flowers are dead silent;
birds are chirping merrily in the verdant valley.

The sun shines at the top of the Cheonil Gazebo,
washing every day in the water flowing into Gugang Port.

While making tea at sunset,
the aroma seeps into the roof tiles of the House;
daily deviations and laziness
are overcome by the words of Dasan.

다산초당 가는 길

다향이 댓잎의 바스락거림에서 깨어난다

뿌리의 길에 적막이 깃들고
돌계단 하나씩 세며 서암을 지난다

음각의 정석을 지켜온 병풍바위를 내려오니
약천의 조롱박에는 동백잎 하나 떠 있다

세월에 뒤틀린 툇마루 앞에 서서 초상화에 묵례 올리니
다조의 물 익어 가는 맛이 어금니에 꽉 낀다

오리 한 마리가 바랜 낙엽을 깔고
연지 폭포가 석가산의 좌돌을 두드린다

백일홍 분홍빛은 죽은 듯이 고요한데
녹음에 젖은 골짜기는 새소리만 청량하다

천일각의 상투머리 잡고 햇빛 혼자 앉아서
구강포 흐르는 물에 속가슴 날마다 씻어 보낸다

노을로 차를 끓이니
곡우차 향이 초당의 기왓장 속으로 들어가고
일상의 일탈과 게으름은
다산 선생님의 말씀으로 모두 녹아내린다

The 38th Main Award of the World Poetry(2024) _ Yoon Jeong-in

■ commentary

The Special Expandability of the Rhymes of Poetry

This year, a female Korean novelist was selected as the winner of the Nobel Prize in Literature. One of the Nobel Prize committee members said in a press conference that her poetic style stands out. Then, what is poetic style? Simply put, it must be a style that makes readers feel the rhyme of a poem. Let's take Yoon Jeong-in's poem as an example. His poem, 'The Way to the House of Dasan', has the following poetic expressions, such as "The aroma of tea wafts with the rustle of reed leaves", "The path of the roots is silent / Counting stone steps, I pass through West Annex", and "Pink zinnia flowers are dead silent / birds are chirping merrily in the verdant valley".

The expression "Pink zinnia flowers are dead silent" is breathtaking. What's more, he adds "Birds are chirping merrily in the verdant valley". Perhaps not many poets know the special expandability of the rhyme of poetry as much as poet Yoon Jeong-in.

- Judges: Won Eung-soon, Park Young-yul, Gwon O-un

■ 심사평

시의 운율이 가지는 특수한 확장성

금년 노벨문학상 수상자로 한국의 한 여류 소설가가 선정된 것에 대한 기자회견에서 노벨상 선정위원회의 한 관계자가 수상작의 문장에 대해, '시적 문체가 돋보인다'고 했다. 새삼스러운 얘기지만 '시적 문체란 무엇인가. 소박하게 말해 '시의 운율이 느껴지는' 문체일 것이다. 예컨대, '다향이 댓잎의 바스락거림에서 깨어난다.' 거나 '뿌리의 길에 적막이 깃들고/ 돌계단 하나씩 세며 서암을 지난다.' (시 「다산초당 가는 길」부분)와 같은 표현은 시적 문체의 대표적일 것이다. 또 있다.

'백일홍 분홍빛은 죽은 듯이 고요한데/ 녹음에 젖은 골짜기는 새소리만 청량하다.' (앞의 작품)

'죽은 듯이 고요한 분홍빛' 도 숨이 막힐 지경인데 거기다가 '녹음에 젖은 골짜기는 새소리가 청량하다' 니! 윤 시인만큼 시의 운율이 가지는 특수한 확장성을 알고 있는 시인도 그리 많지는 않으리라.

－심사위원: 원응순, 박영률, 권오운(글)

The Publication Ceremony for the 41st Anthology of World Poetry
The 37th World Poetry Award Ceremony

- 일시 : 2023년 12월 20일(수) 오후 3시 30분
- 장소 : 마포구 합정동 주민센터 3층
- 주최 : 세계시문학회 • 후원 : 을지출판공사 · 한국수력원자력(주) 한빛원자력본부

국민의례 _ World Poetry 출판기념회 및 세계시문학상 시상식

인사말 _ 세계시문학회 박영률 회장

심사보고 _ 세계시문학회 오진환 명예회장

경과보고 _ 세계시문학회 남창희 부회장

축사 _ 손해일 국제펜 한국본부 이사장(전)

축사 _ 세계시문학회 홍춘표 부회장

진행 _ 세계시문학회 윤수아 사무총장

세계시문학상 대상을
수상하고 소감을 피력하는
구명숙 시인

시상자 박영률 회장과
하객들

세계시문학상 본상을
수상하고 소감을 피력하는
김영선 시인

시상자 박영률 회장과
하객들
▼

세계시문학상 본상을
수상하고 소감을 피력하는
한택규 시인

시상자 박영률 회장과
하객들

시낭송 _ 가나다순

시낭송 _ 김민경 시인

시낭송 _ 김의식 시인

시낭송 _ 명노석 시인

시낭송 _ 박윤기 시인

시낭송 _ 서근희 시인

시낭송 _ 윤 자 시인

시낭송 _ 윤정인 시인   시낭송 _ 장동석 시인

시낭송 _ 주정현 시인   시낭송 _ 최순애 시인

시낭송 _ 최인경 시인   시낭송 _ 형정희 시인

제43차 정기총회

■ 일시 : 2024년 2월 29일 (목)   ■ 장소 : 서울 합정동 들풀

인사말 _ 박영률 회장

감사보고 _ 이규익 감사

진행 _ 윤수아 사무총장

2024 봄 문학기행

■ 일시 : 2024. 5. 30   ■ 장소 : 강원도 영월(청령포, 장릉, 김삿갓유적지 일원)

2024 임원회의

■ 일시 : 2024년 8월 28일(수)   ■ 장소 : 서울 합정동 투썸

2024 가을 문학기행

■ 일시 : 2024년 10월 17일 (목)   ■ 장소 : 충주 수안보파크호텔

문학특강 _ 윤춘식 교수

세계시문학 42집 발간을 축하합니다

서근희 시집

햇살의 향기

올 가을 높은 하늘은 좀 더 힘차게 살아보라고
당부하는 것 같네요.
시를 좋아해 읽으면서 즐거웠지만 시를 쓴다는 작업엔
용기가 필요하고 안간힘을 써 봅니다
인생을 성실히 살아야겠다는 마음은 내 인생의
몫이기도 하지만 나의 시의 몫이기도 합니다.

— 햇살의 향기 「시인의 말」 중에서

세계시문학 42집 발간을 축하합니다

정안야(Anja Jhung) 시집

영원한 그 집

　　정안야의 시는 자신의 일상사에 시적 시선이 집중되고 있음을 보게 된다. 별스런 자극 없이 반복되는 일상을 무의미하게 지나치는 것이 아니라 자기의 일상을 진지하게 음미하면서 삶을 진솔하게 탐색해 나가는 경향성을 보이고 있다는 점이다. 깊이 성찰된 자신의 삶에 관한 시적 반응이 일생생활의 지평에서 운명처럼 조우하는 모습이다.

― 김성열 평론가의 「작품해설」에서

세계시문학 42집 발간을 축하합니다

윤정인 시집

다산초당 가는 길

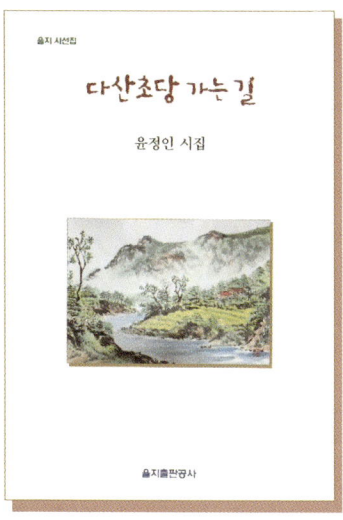

　윤 시인의 작품 세계가 낯선 용어들이 남발되는 도시가 아니고 만덕산 기슭의 초당이고 농촌이면서 그런 친근한 용어가 효율적으로 잘 쓰이고 있기 때문에 공감도가 높다.
　이런 공간적 특성과 함께 다산초당을 중심 소재로 삼았다면 이는 우리가 존경하고 흠모하는 인물로서의 매력뿐만 아니라 글 읽는 소리 외에 슬픈 사랑의 통곡 소리마저 절실하기 때문에 가슴을 깊이 찌를 수밖에 없다.

― 김우종 평론가의 「해설」에서

세계시문학 42집 발간을 축하합니다

살아온 기적이
살아갈 기적이 되다

사람을 낚는 어부

오진환

나는 누구일까?
봄비를 맞으며
나는 누구일까?
소명에 응답하는
체험을 통한 우리
어부 되게 하신 이
빈 삶의 모습 속에
늘 그림자로 오시는
귀한 사명 감당하는 나
사람 낚는 어부 되리라.

김종기 제12시집

시간과 함께
머문 자리

김종기 시인은 시적 대상에 대한 깊은 관찰과 사랑의 시각으로 사유思惟하고, 두뇌 속에서 형상화하고 있다. 그러기 때문에 잠언적箴言的 깨달음과 일깨움으로 깊은 감동의 특징을 지니고 있다.

— 최규창 시인의 「해설」에서

세계시문학 42집 발간을 축하합니다

주정현 제2시집
시인은 시를 쓰고 꿈을 꾼다

주정현 시인은 그리움이 사무치는 고향에 대한 생각의 깊이와 부모님에 대한 잊지 못할 그리움이 여러 자연과 사물 속에서 형상화되어 나타나며 직유보다는 은유가 많아서 더욱 시적 감흥이 크다고 하겠다.

– 박영률 박사의 「평설」에서

한택규 서각작품집
하늘의 말씀에 밑줄을 치고

아송 시인의 근면성과 꾸준한 노력은 그가 마라톤선수로 달리면서 필연적으로 감내한 인내의 한 결실이라고도 할 수 있을 것이다. 특히, 스승을 찾아 사사한 것도 없이 스스로 일군 열정과 성실과 근면의 그만의 짙은 땀으로 이문 작품들이기에 더욱 돋보인다.

– 김춘식 시인의 「추천사」에서

세계시문학 42집 발간을 축하합니다

김민경 제4시집
산허리에 걸린 그림자

김민경 시인의 詩는 언어라는 바탕 위에 기독교 세계관을 갖고, 선교의 봉사활동으로 사랑을 실천하며 느낀 감상을 이미지로 형상화했다. 또한, 삶의 현장에서 체득한 지혜로 그리움이 묻어나고, 많은 군중 속에서도 고독이 넘쳐나는 시구를 찾아 감각적으로 표현한 언어의 향기가 무척 곱고 아름답다. 매우 의미 있는 詩를 쓰는 시 솜씨가 언어를 배합하는 연술사 같다.
- 장동석 시인의 「응원의 글」에서

4인 4색 동시집
넷이서 숨바꼭질

정명희 시인

2024년은 뜻깊은 해입니다. 한국동요의 아버지 윤극영 선생이 온 국민이 즐겨 부르는 동요 〈반달〉, 〈설날〉, 〈고드름〉 등을 발표한 지 100년이 되는 해이기 때문입니다. 이에 발맞춰 국민동요 〈오빠 생각〉의 시인 최순애 선생의 고향 수원에서 2024 세계방정환학술대회를 여는 것은 크게 환영할 일입니다. 이를 기념하기 위해 수원을 대표하는 윤수천, 금금아, 임옥순, 정명희 아동문학가 동심으로 빚은 『넷이서 숨바꼭질』을 펴냈습니다. 읽을수록 정감 있는 4인 4색의 동시집 출간에 축하의 꽃다발을 보냅니다.
- 박상재(한국아동문학인협회 이사장, 문학박사)

넷이서 숨바꼭질을 하면 어떤 재미난 일이 일어날까요? 한 명은 술래가 되고, 나머지 셋은 꼭꼭 숨어야 하겠지요? 우리 문학도 이처럼 '찾는 마음'과 '숨는 마음'들이 서로 어울려 피는 예술이라고 봅니다. 네 분의 빛깔 모두 수놓은 동시집 속에서 많은 어린이들이 숨바꼭질하며 놀러 오시길 기대합니다. - 정경희(방정환연구소 이사장)

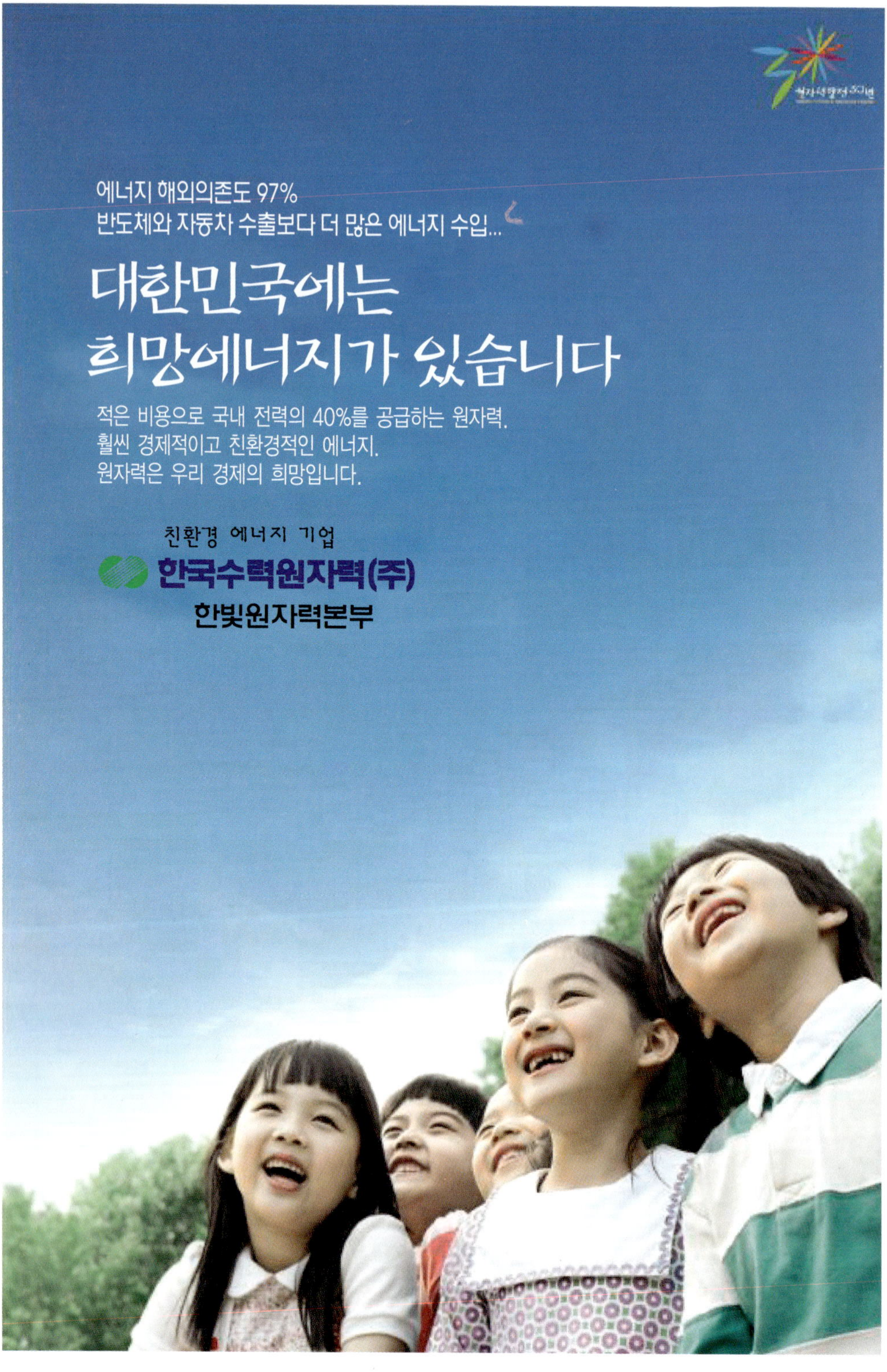

에너지 해외의존도 97%
반도체와 자동차 수출보다 더 많은 에너지 수입...

대한민국에는
희망에너지가 있습니다

적은 비용으로 국내 전력의 40%를 공급하는 원자력.
훨씬 경제적이고 친환경적인 에너지.
원자력은 우리 경제의 희망입니다.

친환경 에너지 기업

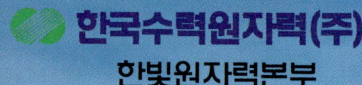

한빛원자력본부

World Poetry

世界詩文學 세계시문학

Vol.42/2024

조기현 작 「꽃에 앉았다 가는 새」

EulJi Publishing Company
을지출판공사
Republic of Korea

WORLD POETRY 世界詩文學 세계시문학
Vol.42 / 2024
(price : US $20)

Published by Park Young-yul

Edited by Kim Hyo-yeol / 김효열
EulJi Publishing Company 을지출판공사
〈등록번호 제 2-741호 1985. 2. 14 등록〉

#603, 41 Yanghwajin-gil, Mapo-gu, Seoul, Korea
TEL 02-334-4050   FAX 02-334-4010
e-mail : ejp4050@hanmail.net

Pubilshed on December 11, 2024. Printed on December 5, 2024

COPYRIGHT : President Park Young-yul

The Society of the World Poetry

#603, 41 Yanghwajin-gil, Mapo-gu, Seoul, Korea
e-mail : wp1982@hanmail.net
Tel. 82-2-334-4050   Mobile 82-10-5253-7932, 82-10-5291-5522

CONTENTS

The 38th Award Winners of the World Poetry(2024)

Seo Keun-hee 서근희 ································· 3
Jhung Anja 정안야 ································· 6
Yoon Jeong-in 윤정인 ································· 9

■ Preface _ Park Young-yul 박영률 ································· 38

■ 영미시 산책 _ Won Eung-soon 원응순
　Come Sleep, Oh Sleep ································· 42

Brazil
Jose de Ribamar Ribeiro ································· 44

Canada
Hédi Bouraoui ································· 46

Dominicana
Lupo Hernández Rueda ································· 48

England

Jacqueline Thévoz · 50
M.E.Spain · 52

España

Jose Gascon Sanchez · 54

France

Georges Friedenkraft · 56

Germany

Hans Dieter Lücke · 58
Jhung Anja · 60

Greece

H.F.Noyes · 64

Italia

Carmelo Bonifacio Malanorino · · · · · · · · · · · · · · · · · 66

Korea

Eom Ki-won 엄기원 · 68
Gwon O-un 권오운 · 70
Jeong Song-jeon 정송전 · 72
Kim Jong-sang 김종상 · 74
Seo Jeong-nam 서정남 · 76

Sohn Hae-il 손해일	78
You Seung-woo 유승우	80
An Geum-sik 안금식	82
Bae Byeong-gun 배병군	86
Bang Jung-sun 방정순	88
Cho Keum-ja 조금자	90
Cho Son-hyong 조선형	92
Choi In-kyung 최인경	94
Choi Sun-ae 최순애	96
Choung Kuy-cha 정귀자	98
Chun Byung-ok 천병옥	100
Chung Chan Woo 정찬우	102
Chung Jee-hong 정지홍	104
Chung Youn-hee 정윤희	108
Go Aeng-ja 고앵자	110
Han Jung-won 한정원	112
Han Man-kyoo 한만규	116
Han Taek-kyu 한택규	118
Hong Chun-pyo 홍춘표	122
Hong Yun-pyeo 홍윤표	124
Hyung Jong-hee 형정희	126
Jang Dong-suck 장동석	128
Jeong Ji-ahn 정지안	132
Jeong Myeong-hee 정명희	134
Jeong Sook-ja 정숙자	138
Jin Sang-soon 진상순	142
Ju Jung-hyun 주정현	144
Kang Hee-seok 강희석	146

Kang Young-duk 강영덕 · 150
Kim Chong-ki 김종기 · 152
Kim Don-young 김돈영 · 154
Kim Eui-sik 김의식 · 156
Kim Hye-sook 김혜숙 · 158
Kim Hyo-yeol 김효열 · 162
Kim Jae-myeoung 김재명 · 164
Kim Jeong-won 김정원 · 166
Kim Jong-hee 김종희 · 170
Kim Min-kyeong 김민경 · 172
Kim Myung-ja 김명자 · 176
Kim Seong-un 김성운 · 180
Kim Young-sun 김영선 · 182
Ko Bang-kyu 고방규 · 184
Koo Myong-sook 구명숙 · 186
Kwon Young-e 권영이 · 188
Lee Byung-seok 이병석 · 192
Lee Chang-soo 이창수 · 194
Lee Eui-young 이의영 · 198
Lee Gyu-ik 이규익 · 202
Lee Han-hee 이한희 · 204
Lee Ok-gyu 이옥규 · 206
Lee Pung-ho 이풍호 · 208
Lee Yong-ho 이용호 · 210
Lim Byeong-jeon 임병전 · 212
Myung No-suk 명노석 · 214
Nam Chang-hee 남창희 · 218
No Jae-ho 노재호 · 220

Oh Jin-hwan 오진환 · 224
Park Kyung-min 박경민 · 226
Park Youn-ki 박윤기 · 230
Park Young-yul 박영률 · 232
Ryu Yong-ha 류용하 · 234
Seo Keun-hee 서근희 · 238
Seong Nag-jung 성낙중 · 240
Shin Dong-myeong 신동명 · 244
Shin Oh-beom 신오범 · 246
Yang Hae-gwan 양해관 · 248
Yeun Kee-young 연기영 · 250
Yoon Hyoung-soon 윤형순 · 254
Yoon Jeong-in 윤정인 · 256
Yoon Yoon-guan 윤윤근 · 260
Yun Ja 윤 자 · 264
Yun Su-a 윤수아 · 266

U.S.A.

Grace Lymm · 268
Jeanne Leigh Schuler · 272
Lenore Cooper Clark · 274
Park In-ae · 276

■ Winners of the World Poetry Awards _ 279
■ History of the Society of the World Poetry _ 284
■ The System of the Society of the World Poetry _ 287

*Preface

With the Delight of Winning the Nobel Prize in Literature

Park Young-yul
President of the Society of the World Poetry

Korean writers have worked hard on writing, and one of them won the Nobel Prize in Literature this year. I congratulate the female writer with pleasure. The fact that poet and novelist, Han Kang, won the Nobel Prize in Literature, which we wanted and waited for, means that she has elevated the status of Korean writers.

Literature is from literary imagination, and so it's sometimes the author's view of life. Philosophy may or may not be related to literature. Literature should be evaluated through literary works. The author's view of life or ethical aspects may influence his or her work, but regardless of that, literature should be evaluated as literature.

As stated in the reason for the selection of the Nobel Prize in Literature, "Han Kang faces the historical trauma and invisible norms in all her works, revealing the fragility of human life in each of her works. She has established herself as an innovator in contemporary prose with her unique perception of the connection between the body and soul, and the living and the dead, and also with her poetic and experimental style."

It has been 24 years since the late President Kim Dae-jung won the Nobel Peace Prize, so it's no wonder that we are thrilled and grateful that she is the first female winner of the Novel Prize in literature in Asia!

Some people criticize her winning the prize negatively, but it is not the right thing to do. It is said that the pen is mightier than the sword. It is a pleasure and an appreciation that Korea can become more known to the world, thanks to her. In particular, I would like to applaud her humble attitude and thoughtful thinking this time.

She said how we can have a party when so many people around the world are dying because of wars. I highly appreciate her consideration for others. I was even more moved by her remark that she celebrated herself, quietly drinking tea with her son. As a writer, I'm just grateful to have realized a lot through her.

I'd like to encourage and applaud poets Seo Keun-hee, Jhung Anja from Germany, and Yoon Jeong-in, who will receive the 38th World Poetry Award this year.

My dear fellow writers of the Society of the World Poetry

Let's hope that we can all write a deeper and higher quality of work, and that more competent translators can greatly contribute to the globalization of Korean literature.

Dec. 11, 2024

■ 권두언

노벨문학상 수상을 기뻐하며

세계시문학회 회장 박 영 률

　문학인이 기지개를 켜니 금년에는 우리나라가 노벨문학상을 수상하게 되어 축하할 일이고 장한 일이며 기쁘기만 하다. 시인이며 소설가인 한강 작가가 원하고 기다렸던 노벨문학상을 수상하게 되었음은 우리 모든 문학인의 위상을 드높인 쾌거다.
　문학은 문학적 상상력이기에 때로는 작가의 인생관이다. 철학이 연관이 될 수도 있지만 그렇지 않을 수도 있음을 안다. 문학은 문학작품을 통하여 평가되어야 할 것이다. 작가의 인생관이나 윤리도덕적인 것이 영향을 나타낼 수도 있지만 그것과 전혀 상관없이 문학은 문학으로 평가되어야 한다.
　노벨문학상 선정 이유에서 밝혔듯이, "한강은 모든 작품에서 역사적 트라우마와 보이지 않는 규범들을 정면으로 마주하며, 각각의 작품에서 인간 삶의 연약함을 드러낸다. 육체와 영혼, 산 자와 죽은 자의 연결에 대한 독특한 인식을 지니고 있으며 시적이고 실험적인 문체로 현대 산문의 혁신가로 자리매김했다."고 밝히고 있다.
 김대중 전 대통령이 노벨평화상을 수상한 후 24년 만의 일이니 그것도 아시아권에서의 첫 여성 수상자라니 어찌 감격하고 감사하지 않을 수 있겠는가!
 혹자는 부정적인 의미의 평가를 하지만 그것은 옳은 일이라고 할 수가 없다. 흔히들 펜은 칼보다 무섭고 강하다고 했는데 이번 한강 작가의 수상으로 대한민국이 전 세계에 크게 알려지게 된 것 자체가 기쁘고 감사할 일이다. 특히 이번 한강 작가의 겸손한 태도와 사려 깊은 생각에 더욱 박수를 보내고 싶다.
 전 세계가 전쟁으로 수많은 사람들이 죽어가고 있는데 무슨 잔치를 하겠느냐는 그 마음이 더욱 귀하다고 믿는다. 조용하게 아들과 차를 마시면서 자축한다는 말이 더더욱 필자를 감동시켰던 것이다. 문학을 하는 사람으로서 많은 것을 깨닫게 되어 감사할 뿐이다.
 금년에 제38회 세계시문학상을 수상하시는 서근희 시인님, 독일 정안야 시인님, 윤정인 시인님께 격려와 박수를 아낌없이 보내 드린다.
 사랑하는 세계시문학회 회원들이여!
 우리 모두 보다 깊고 높은 작품의 메시지를 바라며 더욱 귀한 번역가들이 많이 배출되어 한국문학을 세계화하는데 크게 이바지할 수 있기를 바라는 마음 간절하다.

2024년 12월 11일

* 영미시 산책

Come Sleep, Oh Sleep

by Sir Philip Sidney(1554-1586) / Tr. by Won Eung-soon

Come sleep, Oh sleep, the certain knot of peace,
The baiting place of wit, the balm of woe,
The poor man's wealth, the prisoner's release,
Th'indifferent judge between the high and low;
With shield of proof shield me from out the prease
Of those fierce darts Despair at me doth throw;
Oh make in me those civil wars to cease;
I will good tribute pay, if thou do so.
Take thou of me smooth pillows, sweetest bed,
A chamber deaf to noise and blind to light,
A rosy garland and a weary head;
And if these things, as being thine by right,
Move not thy heavy grace, thou shalt in me,
Livelier than elsewhere, Stella's image see.

[Note] knot of peace: 평화의 매듭/ baiting place: 안식처(resting place)/ balm of woe: 비애의 진정제/ poor man's wealth: 가난한 자의 지산/ prisoner 's release: 죄수의 해방/ indifferent judge: 공정한(impartial) 재판관/ with shield of proof(proved steel): 단련된 강철의 방패로/ shield me: 나를 보호하라(명령문)/ the prease(crowd) of those fierce darts: 맹렬한 화살의 많은 공격/ in me those civil wars: 내 마음의 저 전쟁(내란)을/ make ~to cease: 끝나게 해 주시오/ good tribute pay: 푸짐한 선물을 바치리라/ a chamber deaf to noise: 소음이 나지 않는 방/ blind to light: 빛이 들지 않는 (방)/ if these things, as being thine by right: 비록 당연히 그대의 것인 이런 것들이/ move not thy heavy grace: 그대의 큰 은혜에 못 미친다 해도/ thou shalt (see Stella's image) in me: 그대는 내 안에서(나에게서) 스텔라의 모습을 보리라/ livelier: 보다 더 생생한/ Stella's image: a dream of Stella(시인의 연인)/ 소네트 형식의 14행 시임.

* 영미시 산책

오라, 잠이여, 오 잠이여

필립 시드시 작 / 원응순 번역

오라, 잠이여! 화평의 확실한 매듭인, 오 잠이여,
위트의 안식처, 비애의 진정제,
빈곤한 자의 재산, 죄수의 해방이여.
귀천을 가리지 않는 공정한 재판관;
단련한 강철의 방패로서 나를 보호하라, 절망이
던지는 숱한 맹렬한 화살의 공격으로부터;
오, 내 마음의 저 전쟁들을 끝나게 해 주시오;
그러면 내가 너에게 푸짐한 선물을 바치리라.
그대는 가지리라, 부드러운 베개와, 향긋한 잠자리와,
조용(아늑)하고, 빛이 들지 않는 침실과,
고달픈 머리에 얹을 장미꽃 다발을:
비록 당연히 그대의 것인 이런 것들이
그대의 큰 은덕에 못 미친다 해도, 그대는 내 안에서 보리라
다른 어디에서보다 생생한 스텔라의 모습을.

Won Eung-soon / Korea

* Poet, Ph.D. Emeritus Prof. of Kyung Hee Univ.
* Chief Editor of The Christian Literature of Korea(Quarterly Magazine)
* Manager & Editor of the Professor's Newspaper
* Elder of Dongsoong Presbyterian Church
* Adviser of the Society of the World Poetry

Brazil/Jose de Ribamar Ribeiro

Let Me Leave

Let me leave through the strange world, my absence
will bring relief to you...
leave me alone... I'm a lost sheep of the flock
that goes vacillating
let me go... Good Bye!

Let me leave in this world drops of sweat on a all my
way, after all, I want to be a hero of the war without
giving vexation, without using the sword...

Let me go to the sun that litlle by little
goes on the horizon
I want to find my place
on the sun, born on this
land, on the sea, wind and mountans...

Let me go... be an adventurer
of the thick woods of the roads that takeme to the
horizon without love and caress.

Jose de Ribamar Ribeiro / Brazil

Rua 16-Quadra 22-Casa 07-Conjunto
Habitacional Turu-Sao Luis-Maranhao-
Brazil

Brazil/Jose de Ribamar Ribeiro

나를 보내 주오

낯선 세상으로 나를 보내 주오 내가 떠나면
그대는 오히려 위안을 얻으리니……
날 홀로 있게 내버려 두오……
망설임의 발길을 옮기는 나는 길 잃은 양(羊)
나를 보내 주오…… 안녕!

내 모든 발길을 적시는 물방울들을
이 세상에 남기고 마침내 나는
고통도 칼도 없는 전쟁의 영웅이 되고파라

차츰차츰 수평선으로 달려가는
태양에게로 나를 보내 주오
이 땅과 바다와 바람과
산들에게서 태어난 나는 태양 위에서
내 자리를 찾고 싶어라……

나를 보내 주오
사랑도 애무도 없이 수평선에 이르는
울창한 숲길을 지나 모험가가 되도록.

The Citadel of our Dreams

The citadel of our dreams
Looms behind
A Rose intertwined
With another Rose

A loving couple
In the foreground
Of our blank page

Exit from the shadows
The sculpture
Maps our future.

Hédi Bouraoui / Canada

4700 Keele Street
North York
Ontario, Canada M3J 1P3

Canada/Hédi Bouraoui

우리 꿈의 성(城)

우리 꿈의 성채는
다른 장미와 뒤엉킨
한 송이 장미 뒤에
희미하게 보인다.

우리의 비어 있는 책장 속의
정원 속에 있는
사랑의 연인들은

그림자로부터 퇴장한다.
그 조각품이
우리의 미래를 그려 놓는다.

Dominicana/Lupo Hernández Rueda

Prayer

Lord, Thou art in all places
forgiving the living and the dead,
always kind, Lord, Thou art like
beautiful orchards for those who are
afficted with sorrows.

Lord, Thou art in every home,
in the feverish flock, in the deserts;
Thou toucheth all harbors with Faith,
Love beneath the heavens and the seas.

Lord who grows inside of men,
Thou hast by virtue a multitude of names.
Lord of Friendship and of Hope.

It is time that Thou fulfillest the
temperance of men, the sons of Earth,
so that there may be peace, an end to war.

Lupo Hernández Rueda / Dominicana

Apartado de Correos 30323
Santo Domingo, Republica
Dominicana

Dominicana / Lupo Hernández Rueda

기도하는 사람

신이시여, 당신은 산 자와 죽은 자를
용서하는 모든 곳에 계시며
언제나 친절하십니다.
신이시여, 당신은 슬픔으로 고통받는
사람들에겐 아름다운 정원과 같습니다.

신이시여, 당신은 모든 가정에 계시며,
열기찬 군중 속에, 사막에 계십니다.
당신은 신념으로 모든 항구를 만지셨고,
사랑은 하늘과 바다 밑에 있습니다.

사람 안에서 자라시는 신이시여,
당신은 미덕에 의해 여러 이름을 가지십니다.
우정과 희망의 주인이시여.

지구의 아들이시여, 당신이
인간의 절제를 완성시키실 시간이 왔습니다.
그래서 평화와 전쟁의 끝이 깃들도록 해 주소서.

England/Jacqueline Thévoz

Give what you like

Since I have saved your life
in the maze of the Seven Wells
you can give what you like:
a rose from the sands
a jasmine flower
the sweetness from palms
of from the leaves of mint,
the flesh of the coconut tree
or camel's milk,
or simply your smile
as bright as the sun that shines
on the cool oasis.
But,
if you have nothing to give
no flower, no fruit, no joy,
nothing at all,
I understand.

Jacqueline Thévoz / England

England/Jacqueline Thévoz

네가 좋아하는 것을 주어라

내가 너의 생명을 구한 이래
일곱 개의 벽으로 된 미궁 속에서
너는 네가 좋아하는 것을 줄 수 있다.
모래밭으로부터 한 떨기 장미를
한 송이 재스민 꽃을
종려나무나 박하잎으로부터 달콤함을
코코아나무의 신선함을
낙타의 우유를
혹은 시원한 오아시스에 비치는 태양처럼
밝고 순박한 너의 미소를
하지만,
네가 만일 아무것도 줄 것이 없다면
꽃도, 과일도, 기쁨도
전혀 아무것도 없더라도
나는 이해한다.

Old Acquaintance

I met my teenage self the other day;
She stepped out the note-books that I'd kept
And looked at me accusingly. Except
In trivialities, there was no way
I'd played the part that she had meant to play.
Hers was a mind unwilling to accept
That dreams could fail, or people prove inept,
Or good intentions suffer feet of clay.
My struggling protestations seemed uncouth.
Contrasted with the simple clarity
With whch her innocence expressed the truth.
The only sign of progress seems to be
That, whereas I admire my clear-eyed youth,
Her understanding couldn't stretch to me.

M.E.Spain / England

Flat 34 Airile House
17 Airlie Gardens LONDON
W8 7AN

England/M.E.Spain

오랜 사귐

나는 언젠가 나 자신의 십대 시절을 만났다.
그녀는 내가 보관했던 공책을 들고 걷고 있었고
나를 나무라듯 보고 있었다.
사소한 것을 제외하고는
그녀가 연기하고자 했던 부분들을
내가 연기할 수 있는 방법은 없었다.
실패했던 꿈들, 또는 인간이 바보라는 것,
좋은 의도가 점토 속에 빠져 고통받는다는 사실을
받아들이고 싶지 않은 마음이었다.
나의 도전적인 항의는
진실을 표현하는 그녀의 순수하고 단순한 명백함과
비교하여 볼 때 투박한 것으로 보였다.
발전과 진보의 단 하나의 표시는
내가 맑은 눈의 젊음을 찬미하는데 비해
그녀의 이해가 나에 미칠 수 없음에 있는 듯 했다.

España/Jose Gascon Sanchez

Living From Illusion

If we worked with honour and sincerity
How marvellous life would be!
Happiness makes mankind smile
To banish hate and wickedness

What does humanity think about?
If it despises the illusion to smile
And prefers to kill... to die,
and afterwards... suffer in Eternity,

Nobody, realises that this is no life,
To have hell in our hands,
And so our life is more than lost.

Why do we hate oneanother, we are brothers,
And God not forgiving nor forgetting,
Because what we are doing is not done by humans.

Jose Gascon Sanchez / España

C/Mayor de Nazaret, 77.
(46024-Valencia)
Espana

España/Jose Gascon Sanchez

환상으로부터의 삶

우리가 훌륭히 그리고 진지하게 일한다면
인생은 얼마나 경이로울 것인가!
행복은 인류에게 웃음을 주고
증오와 사악을 떨쳐 주리니

인류는 무엇을 생각하는가?
그것이 환상의 미소를 멸시하고
죽고 죽이기를 좋아하는 것이라면
그리고 난 후 영원 속에서 괴로워하게 되는 것이라면

아무도 이것을 삶이라 하지 않으리
손 안에 지옥을 쥐고
우리 인생은 깊은 절망이 되리.

왜 서로 미워하는가. 형제들이여
신은 용서하지도 잊지도 않으리
우리가 행하는 것이 인간의 그것이 아니므로.

France/ Georges Friedenkraft

Embrace

I have known the brief happiness of the embrace

You have come from over the ink and the salt
My dream beyond the horizon
From over the verdant slopes of the volcanoes
Where corollas of orchids
Reach out like pink fists
And perfume the heavy dampness
You have come from beyond the Indonesian seas
Where the tepid foam of waves
Caress gently the fisherman's outrigger
From over Borneo and its blowpipes
The bamboo grown thick like leaden sheaves.

You have come from over the desert
My transcontinental love
From over the parched steppes
Where the ancient stream of Mongolian cohorts
Had ravaged the wild grass in the Siberian wind
From over the lakes with extravagant shell-fish
And the majestic descent of a certain meteor

- Translation: W.H.Goh-Chapouthier

Georges Friedenkraft / France

11 Bis Rve du Val de Grace 75005 Paris, France

France/ Georges Friedenkraft

포옹

나는 포옹의 덧없는 행복을 알았다.

그대는 잉크와 소금 너머로부터 왔고
수평선 너머의 내 꿈은
화산의 푸릇푸릇한 경사면 너머로부터 왔다.
난초의 꽃봉오리가
마치 분홍 손가락처럼 펼쳐지고
깊은 습지로 향기를 내뿜는 듯한 그곳으로부터
그대는 인도네시아의 바다를 건너왔나니.
따스한 포말이
어부의 돛대를 부드럽게 어루만지는 그곳
납 묶음처럼 두껍게 자란
대나무 취관(吹管)이 있는 보루네오로부터.

그대는 사막으로부터 왔나니
대륙을 건너온 내 사랑
바싹 말라붙은 걸음걸음으로
고대 몽고 보병대의 행렬이
시베리아의 바람 속에서 들판을 휩쓴 곳으로부터
화려한 조개가 살고
이름 모를 유성의 웅대한 추락이 있는 호수로부터,

Germany/Hans Dieter Lücke

Horses

Symmetry of motion,
unattainably tender
looseness of limbs,
classic stretching of bodies,
of rearing tails,
spontaneous pas de quatre of hoofs,
fleeing manes in the flying wind:
individuality used to flights;
skill to survive since millenniums,
original harmony in perfection,
culmination of a creation
which melt away us in our hands.

Hans Dieter Lücke / Germany

Winklertr. 4 a
1000 Berlin 33
Tel. 030/891 57 83

Germany/Hans Dieter Lücke

말[馬]

동작의 균정(均整)
무한히 부드럽고
시원스러운 사지(四肢),
고전적으로 쭉 뻗은 동체(胴體),
위로 솟구친 꼬리,
자동적으로 움직이는 네 개의 발굽들,
훗날리는 바람결에 도망치는 갈기털:
도망치는 개성(個性)
수천 년 전부터 오래오래 살아 남은 비결,
완성 속에 이미 예정된 조화
우리의 두 손 밑에서 녹아 버리는
어떤 창조의 정점(頂点).

I Will Bloom

I walk along the field edge path.

In the green field,
there are many grass flowers in bloom
that have braved snow and rain.

I quietly
carry the flowers
into my mind.

Each grass flower of its own style
is really pretty;

Jhung Anja / Germany

* 8th president of the Korean Writers Society in Germany
* advisory committee member of the Korean Nurses Association in Germany
* debuted as a poet in 2015 through the magazine, *The Literary Trend*
* debuted as an essayist through the magazine, *The Spring of Literature*
* debuted as a novelist through the magazine, *The Literary Trend*
* member of International PEN/Korean Center
* collection of her poems: *The Eternal House*
* collection of her short stories: *Bells Ringing at Noon*

Germany/Jhung Anja

fascinated by their various scents,
I want to get away
from my daily routine.

Even in a world as heavy as a rock,
even in a noisy world,
spring comes after winter;
winter goes again
and spring comes again.

Just like the flowers,
I want to bloom again,
smelling nice.

Like the flowers in that field,
I will bloom.

- translated by Woo Hyeong-sook

꽃 피우리라

풀섶 들길을 걷는다

푸르른 저 들판
그동안 눈비 맞으며
소담히 피워 낸 꽃송이 송이들

조용히
내 안에
고이 옮겨 심는다

제멋에 겨운
풀꽃들
오색향기에 취해
얽매였던 낡은 삶을
슬며시 풀어놓고 싶다

바위처럼 무거운 세상
소란스런 세상
겨울 가고 봄 오고
다시 겨울 가고
또 봄이 오듯이

Germany / Jhung Anja

다시 한 번
새순 돋아 보리라
향기롭게 돋게 하리라

저 들판의 꽃들처럼
나도 꽃 피우리라

Peace Flow

Think of Milton's 'opening eyelids
of morn,' Aurora's spreading aura
tendering warmth to night-chiled earth,
imparting to stone an animate flush,
brushing each bush, upflowing to light
the loftiest mountain rim and crest
And think of the closing lids at dusk-
the way the evening shadows creep
across the sun-scorched plain and pasture,
cooling and soothing with healing rest.
So peace will come-thus irresistibly-
will make its move with the certain sweep
of vesper shade and day glow,
woo us like breath of life in wake if war-
as after near-death being resurrects.

H.F.Noyes / Greece

C/O MINK Productions
10, Dimokritou, Kolonaki
Athens, GREECE 10673

Greece/H.F.Noyes

평화의 강

아침의 눈꺼풀을 여는 밀턴
밤의 한기로 차가워진 대지를 녹이며
돌멩이에 홍조의 생기를 전하고
수풀들을 스치고 지나
높은 산, 가장자리와 꼭대기를 밝히려
새벽을 여는 오로라를 생각하라
해 질 무렵 눈꺼풀의 닫힘 —
편안한 휴식으로 시원하게 어루만져 주며
태양이 작열하는 평원과 목초지로
저녁 그림자가 기어 드는 길을 생각하라
그리하여 평화는 찾아올 것이다 — 불안하게 —
초저녁 그림자와 달아오른 하루를 일소하여
그 움직임을 시작할 것이며
평화는, 죽어 가는 이가 부활한 후처럼 —
전쟁의 자국을 좇아 생명의 숨결같이 우리에게 사랑을 호소하리

Italia / Carmelo Bonifacio Malanorino

Woman of Flowers

When the universe colours up
of yous pure morning water-lily,
of the divine smile one has an idea
that dresses the world with the sweet dawn;

and you appear in a dream that decorates you
with light like our humble goddess
that from her pure chalice she delights herself
that the world loves with sweetness.

Daughter of the sun and the earth, sound
of harp that releases apotheosis naked
of sweetness that around her whispers;

and enchants the eyes more than a star and inspires
the music of shining kingdoms
that inside the heart maybe they are eternal.

Carmelo Bonifacio Malanorino / Italia

Italia / Carmelo Bonifacio Malanorino

꽃의 여인

그대의 순수한 아침 수련으로,
달콤한 새벽으로 세상을 장식하려는 자의
성스런 미소로
세상이 붉게 물들면;

우리의 초라한 여신처럼 빛으로 그대를 장식하고,
그녀의 순결한 성(聖)으로 기쁨에 겨워
달콤하게 세상이 사랑을 나누는
그런 꿈속에서 그대는 나타난다.

태양과 지구의 딸
하프가 성스런 소리를 내고
그녀의 속삭임을 달콤하게 감싼다;

그리고 아마도 영원히 가슴속에 있을,
빛나는 왕국의 음악에 영감을 주고
별들보다 더 많은 사람들을 황홀하게 하는 그대가 있다.

Good Names

'Father'
By the name only,
He becomes the sky
To my family.

We can stretch our wings,
Like birds that fly as freely as they want.

'Mother'
By the name only,
She becomes a nest
For my family.

We can fold our wings,
Like birds that fall into a warm sleep.

Eom Ki-won / Korea

* Writer of Children's Literature
* President of Korean Children's Literature Association
* Adviser of the Society of the World Poetry
* The Counselor the Society of the World Poetry of the World Poetry
* Published 15children's poetry collections including *A Home Where Baby is Growing* and *A Baby and A Goat*

Korea/엄기원

좋은 이름

'아버지'
그 이름만으로도
우리 가족에겐
하늘이다

우리는 날개를 펴고
마음대로 날 수 있는 새들이다

'어머니'
그 이름만으로도
우리 가족에겐
보금자리다

우리는 날개를 접고
포근히 잠들 수 있는 새들이다.

Korea/Gwon O-un

Backyard

Two cicadas are paired together;
the low branch of the persimmon tree droops down.

The male cicada, making loud buzzing noises,
hangs on to the tail of the female cicada;
the persimmon tree sways and sweats.

That cry can't be buried anywhere;
as if buttoning up the lower parts,
sticking firmly,
they mate and fly away.

As if they see a faint hope,
emitting droplets of urine,
they fly to the bright backyard.

- translated by Woo Hyeong-sook

Gwon O-un / Korea

* debuted as a poet from the literary contest of the Chosun Daily Newspaper in 1966
* member of literary groups, the Shinchun Poetry and the Poetics
* former editorial journalist of the magazine for students, *the Hakwon*
* former editorial director of the Female Encyclopedia of KBS
* professor at Dept. of Creative Writing of Jungang University
* adviser of the Society of the World Poetry
* collection of poems: *Correcting the Korean Language*, and many more

Korea / 권오운

뒤란

매미 두 마리가 쌍으로 붙어서
먹감나무 낮은 가지가 휘우듬하다

세상 울음 다 무리꾸럭한 수컷이
암컷 꽁무니에 매달리자
꿈틀 먹감나무가 땀을 흘린다

저 울음 어디 다 묻을 수가 없어서
아랫도리를 개씹단추 채우듯
단단히 찌른 채
어부랭이 하고 날아간다

실낱같은 저희 길이 보인다는 듯이
이슬 오줌 지리며
환한 뒤란으로 날아간다.

Korea/Jeong Song-jeon

A shadow

The farewell is
Maybe bubblelike.

Sitting in the shadow of love
Even though spread out the sky like petals
It is unable to cover the space of life.

Being a standstill in childhood
It's a wrinkled skirt of monologue
When coming back from the outside, and open the door,
The flowers of perception pour out and

Even so
The farewell is
With an indelible look
Like a shadowy something.

- Tr. by Shin Mi-ja

Jeong Song-jeon / Korea

* Debuted with *Poems and Poetics* in 1962
* Received and graduated master's degree from Joong-ang University
* Served as the president of Literary Society of the World Poetry
* Awardee of Korea Free Poet Association, and many more
* Collections of Poems: *The words of the wind*, etc.
* Collection of poems for appreciation: *Backwaters of my life*, etc.
* Korean-English Poems: *Walking with you*, etc.

Korea/정송전

그림자

이별이란 게
어쩌면 거품 같은 거.

사랑의 그늘에 앉아
하늘을 꽃잎처럼 펼쳐도
삶의 공간은 가려지지 않는 거.

유년으로 멈춰 있는
독백의 주름치마
외출에서 돌아와 방문을 열면
인식의 꽃이 쏟아지고

그래도
이별이란 건
시선이 지워지지 않는
그림자 같은 거.

Korea/Kim Jong-sang

A Discarded Old Tire

How hard did that tire work
until it gets that old?

Until recently for people,
I am sure it ran every single day,
carrying heavy loads.

On a muddy road or a gravel field,
it had to run, as if being whipped.
Though it worked without a break,
it's thrown away now, because it's old.

Like old people in a senior citizen center,
it is stuck in the garbage,
where there are rotten or broken-down things.

Now it's clear where it's going to go.
However, it has a faint hope
that it may be given something to do.

- translated by Woo Hyeong-sook

Kim Jong-sang / Korea

* born in 1935 in Andong
* debuted as a novelist in 1958 through the magazine, *The New Classroom*
* debuted as a poet through winning the Annual Literary Contest of the Seoul Newspaper
* collection of his poems: *Mom with Dirt on Her Hands*, etc.
* literary award: the Korean Literary Award, the Sowol Literary Award, etc.

Korea/김종상

폐타이어

얼마나 힘들게 살았을까
저렇게 낡아질 때까지

사람을 위해 이날까지
무거운 짐을 받쳐 싣고
매일 빠짐없이 달렸겠지

진창길이고 자갈밭이고
가리지 않고 채찍을 맞으며
숨 가쁘게 일만 하다가
낡았다고 이제는 버려져

경로당에 모인 노인네처럼
썩은 고물들만 모인 자리에
쓰레기로 한몫 끼인 타이어

이제는 갈 곳이 분명한데도
또 무슨 할 일이 주어질까
실낱같은 희망을 품고 있다.

Ch'oso

The wind blowing in the field of soybeans
Cooled the heat of the earth all too soon

Birds in the fields of sorghum
Fly away busily

Loved things of mindless like wind
And things of changes like cloud

Whispering something
With all its might

Leaving behind things of nostalgic sweetness,
Things that sunk deep in one's mind

So, it is like summer
That glides by heartlessly

Seo Jeong-nam / Korea

* member of Korea writers' association
* member of Korean modern poetry writers' association, a member of international pen club in Korea headquarters, second chairman of Seocho literary men's association, chairman of Chongda literary men's association, chairman of Korea psychology counsel association, an honorary Doctor of Literature and so on.
* poet, a pastor, a judicial scrivener, a counselor of psychology and so on
* advisory Committee member of the Society of the World Poetry

Korea/서정남

처서(處暑)

콩밭에 이는 바람
어느새 지열을 식히고

산그늘 수수밭
새들도 바쁘게 날아간다.

바람처럼 무심한 것과
구름처럼 변전하는 것들을

무어라 그리도
혼신으로 사랑하다가

못 견디게 그리운 것과
사무치게 한스러운 것들을 그대로 두고

여름이 가듯 그렇게
차마 그렇게 떠날 수는 없거늘

Korea/Sohn Hae-il

When I Am A Tree's Leaf

Spring, drawn barely through the water pipe
From your unexhausted well,
Jororong Jororong
A love budding in the light green leaf.
Spent its summer unnoticed,
A white blood corpuscle is dying in harassed by wordly waves.

Every time when the leaves are grown yellow colored,
They have gray hair appear one by one,
The more their annual rings are cleared,
Their contritions increase one by one,
But now I have to live,
Loving the hateful by degrees.

My mental vision is clouded up by an idle greed,
Wiping the frosts of my mind in blowing up "Ho, Ho",
I have to live like the fresh trees,
And again I have to live, only with a fresh yearning,
Stretching their branched toward the sunlights.

-Translated by Won Eung-soon

Sohn Hae-il / Korea

*Graduated from Seoul National Univ. from Dept. of National Language, Graduate School of Hongik Univ.(Ph.D. 1991).
*First Debut as a New Poet through the <Simunhak>, 1978
*Poetic Anthology: <Ddeudabang A Magpie's House>, etc.
*Won a Prize of 'the University Literature', that of 'the Simunhak', and that of 'the Sowolmunhak', etc.
*<Present> A Honorable Chief Director of International PEN Korea Headquarters, a Councilor of the Modern Poetic Association of Korea, a Director of the Literary Association of Korea, and that of the General Graduates' Seoul National Univ., etc.

Korea/손해일

내가 하나의 나뭇잎일 때

마르지 않는 당신의 샘에서
겨우내 물관으로 길어 올린 봄
쪼로롱 쪼로롱
연초록 잎새에 촉 트던 사랑
어느새 여름도 다 가고
세파에 시달려 죽어가는 흰 피톨.

잎파랑이가 노오랗게 이울 때마다
새치도 하나씩 늘고
나이테가 선명해질수록
후회도 하나씩 늘지만
이제는
미운 것들도 조금씩 사랑하며 살아야지.

부질없는 욕심으로 흐려지는 시야
호오~ 호오~
마음에 낀 성에를 닦으며
풋나무처럼 살아야지
늘 햇살 쪽으로만 가지를 뻗어
싱싱한 그리움으로 살아야지.

Moonlight Study · 29

Dangling on a winter branch. moonlight is laughing.
Coming along with the light, the wind is crying together.
Glittering and scattered white
Like broken pieces of glass,
Winter pain
Heaped up in my heart
Becomes a cold never to be healed.
My sister, widowed when twenty-four
And leading her life till sixty.
Her long suffering coughs
Echoes all winter
From the deepest bottom of my heart.

You Seung-woo / Korea

* debut as a poet in 1966 through the Modern Literature
* former president of the Korean Modern Poets Association
* member of the advisory board of the Korean Writers Association
* advisor of International PEN Korean Center
* received the Kyunghee Literature Award, etc
* collections of his poems: 11 collections, including Wind Variations
* books: six books, including Comments on Korean Poems
* published his autobiography, The Poet Yu Seung-woo

Korea/유승우

달빛 연구 · 29

달빛이 겨울가지에 걸려 웃고 있다.
바람이 따라와 같이 운다.
유리조각처럼 반짝이며
하얗게 흩어지는
겨울의 아픔.
내 가슴속에 쌓여
낫지 않는 감기가 된다.
스물네 살에 홀어미 되어
예순까지 살아온 누님의
해묵은 기침 소리가
내 가슴속 저 밑창에서
겨우내 올려오고 있다.

Korea/An Geum-sik

Yeoju Ssangyong

Torrential rain swept across the Yeoju area,
cutting deep grooves through the Eastern Flat Rock.

Old wherry men
rowed hard on the Yeo River,
till winter deepened.

Even kerosene lamps dozed off
in the mountain villages,
Heonbau Village and Bomseot Village,
near the Yeo River in dreamy winter.

Moving his shoulders up and down,
old wherry men danced
when two villages were in a bitter tug-of-war,
just like a fierce battle of two dragons 「-」.

An Geum-sik / Korea

* debuted as a poet through the magazine, "The Hanmaek"
* served as an advisory committee member of Gyeonggi Province
* served as a director of Yeoju Cultural Center
* board member of the Society of the World Poetry
* vice president of the General Allies for Righteous Army Memorial Works

Korea/안금식

The mountains echoed back their drum beats;
each leader kept shouting "Sul-lyeong-su!".
Twelve dancing kids and some 400 participants
made us win the Presidential Award.
Oh Yeoju Ssangyong Tug-of-War*!
At last the game
is now listed on the National Archives of Korea.

　* Poet An Geum-sik, the head of Yeoju Cultural Center in 1989, led the event.

- translated by Woo Hyeong-sook

Korea/An Geum-sik

여주 쌍용 대통령상

억수장마 하우처
동대(東臺)의 암석 골이 패이고

늙은 사공 여강 아라리로
거룻배 흘떠 가다가
겨울이 깊어질 양이면

산촌의 호롱불조차
깜빡! 졸음 겨웁던
흔바우마을, 봄섯마을
꿈꾸는 겨울 여강

늙은 사공 께끼춤
어깨 으쓱이고
쌍용줄 휘돌아 치던
해나무 아래 「-」

Korea/안금식

북소리 산메아리 아득한
술령수! 술령수! 또 술령수
열두 무동(舞童), 출연진 4백여 명이
대통령상 일궈 낸
여/주/쌍/용 큰줄다리기*
마침내
국가 기록원에도 등재되었다네

*1989년도 당시 여주문화원장 안금식 시인 총괄

Korea/Bae Byeong-gun

God's Choice

My mom has told my younger sister
that it's her wish to die early,
not wanting to make her children suffer,
not wanting to live long to be useless.

My younger sister has told my mother
that it's her wish to see Mom live to the age of 100,
as it's not hard to take care of Mom, rather happiness,
and Mom is not a useless person but a precious person.

If my mom's wish comes true and she dies early.
my heart will be broken, as I can't see her again.
If she lives to the age of 100, as my sister wishes,
I'll be sad, as Mom has terminal pancreatic cancer.

I understand both my mother and younger sister,
but I'm sorry I can't fully agree with either of them.
I wish Mom would live a few more years without pain.
Ah! Whose wish will God grant?

- translated by Woo Hyeong-sook

Bae Byeong-gun / Korea

* vice director of the Society of the World Poetry
* board member of the Korean Songwriters Association
* guidance committee member of the Asian and Pacific Writers Association
* ethics committee member of the Korean New Literature Association

Korea/배병군

하나님의 선택

어머니께서 여동생에게 말씀하셨네
일찍 죽는 것이 소원이라고
자식들 고생 안 시키고 빨리 죽고 싶다고
쓸데없이 오래 살고 싶지 않다고

여동생이 어머니께 말씀드렸네
엄마가 백 세까지 사는 것이 소원이라고
엄마 돌보는 것 힘 안 들고 행복하다고
엄마는 쓸데없는 사람이 아니라 소중한 사람이라고

어머니의 소원이 이루어져 일찍 돌아가시면
제대로 효도 못 한 것과 다시는 뵐 수 없어 내 맘 아프고
여동생의 소원이 이루어져 백 세까지 사시면
췌장암 말기인 어머니께서 힘드실 것 같아 내 맘 아프네

어머니의 마음도 여동생의 마음도 이해가 되지만
나는 누구의 소원도 전적으로 들어줄 수 없어 안타깝네
나의 소원은 어머니께서 고통 없이 몇 년만 더 사시는 것
아! 하나님은 과연 누구의 소원을 들어주실까?

Korea/Bang Jung-sun

A Silkworm's Life

Wiggling, tossing and turning,
it sees the sky beginning to brighten.
It reaches a green field, nibbling leaves all its life.
Thunder and lightning may startle it
when I think about eyes and ears.
After its first moult, second moult, third and fourth moult,
it has a big appetite in a new outfit.
Wriggling under green sheets, it spends time.
Seven to eight days pass by,
and its body becomes dull and brown.
Praying to heaven with a dream, it finds a haven.
Wrapped in the cocoon of thousands of strands,
it becomes immovable and rests in it.
Trying with weak power for the next generation,
it opens the door to get out.
As it produces offspring with its partner,
flowers gather and rumble on it.
"Hey, grow up well and open the way to the universe."
With the words, it flaps the wings and ends its life.
A silkworm's life is like that.

- translated by Woo Hyeong-sook

Bang Jung-sun / Korea

* board member of the Society of the World Poetry
* She debuted through the monthly magazine, *The Literary Movement & Trend*
* collection of poems: *A Snipe Beside the Beach*, etc
* literary awards: the Main Prize of the World Poetry, etc.
*Address: 360, jaryong-ri, Sangha-myeon, Gochang-gun, Jeonbuk, Korea

Korea/방정순

누에의 일생

꼼지락거리다 뒤척이다
날이 밝아 푸른 들에
도달하여 전생을 갉아먹다
천둥 번개 소리 깜짝하며
내가 귀가 있고 눈이 있어
스르르 한 잠 두 잠 서너 잠에 깨어나
헌옷 벗고 새 옷 갈아입으니 식욕은 왕성하다
푸른 이불 속을 뒤척이다 세월이 가니
어느덧 칠팔일
몸은 둔해지고 누른빛은 꿈을 그리고
하늘 향해 기도하며 안식처를 찾는다.
수천 가닥 실타래 풀어 몸을 감싸니
움직일 수 없는 몸 안식하다
이세를 위해 연약한 힘으로 문을 여니
나갈 수 있는 문이 열려
동반자와 이세를 남기고 보니
꽃들이 모여 웅성이니
애들아 성장하여 우주에 길 열어라 하고
날개 퍼덕이며 생을 마감한다.
누에의 일생은 이러하다.

Korea/Cho Keum-ja

Ode to Cosmos Flowers

Fluffy white clouds in the blue sky;
cuckoos crying somewhere in the woods;
cosmos flowers swaying on the riverside.

The memories I love;
missing my love, with flowers in my hair,
I want to go somewhere with white cloud friends.

Under the indigo blue sky, in the gentle wind,
cosmos flowers wave their thin necks, welcoming me.
Thanks to you, cosmos, I like autumn, feeling good.

You wave your hands. welcoming this passer-by.
I want to stay with you for a long time,
but I'll keep you deep in my heart instead.

- translated by Woo Hyeong-sook

Cho Keum-ja / Korea

* debuted as a poet in 2005 through the magazine, "The Literary Trend"
* graduated from the graduate school of Wonkwang University
* first prize in a female essay contest hosted by Seohai Broadcasting Company
* received an award of 40 years service for the Red Cross society
* received an award for her filial piety
* collection of poems: "A Treasure Put in a Pottery"

Korea/조금자

코스모스 예찬

파란 하늘엔 솜털 같은 흰 구름
숲속 어디선가 뻐꾸기 울음소리
강변 길가엔 한들거리며 핀 코스모스

내가 사랑하는 추억들
님 그리며 꽃잎 따 머리에 꽂고
흰 구름 벗 삼아 어디론가 가고 싶다.

쪽빛 하늘 살랑이는 바람 속에
가녀린 목 흔들며 반겨 주는 코스모스
네가 있기에 가을이 즐겁고 좋다.

오가는 길손 손 흔들어 환영하니
오래도록 네 곁에 머물고 싶지만
내 가슴속에 깊이 간직하리라.

Korea / Cho Son-hyong

Before the Judge

    At the beginning of one spring, I need the clothes to cover my naked body from long, long ago; It's because, in summer, a fig tree of wide leaves in Eden can conceal Myself. And, from now on, thinking of not being uncovered by anybody, I hid all that I had belonged to. But, in autumn, what I had in mind are, I feel, getting nerves for fear of one or two being found.
People gathered together in twos and threes in the plaza.
Before them at last came the Last day of the Judgement.
There were
Wind,
Sunlight,
And water in there:
But, as they could not be the real judge, I had no choice but to wait.
On a rainy day of autumn leaves, I came out to the plaza
And couldn't help surrendering.
" O Lord, I'm naked! in the end"

Winter is like a mirror.
I stand in front of Him in a shameful look.

Cho Son-hyong / Korea

* First Debut as a Poet from the Monthly *the Munhaksege* (Literary World) With a Prize of a new Poet(1993)
* Literary Works: *At the Lake the Train Stopped too, A sluice, The Waterway*(Anthology in English),
* Prose Collection: *Morning of a Zelkova Tree*
* Member of the Korean Writers' Association
* (The former) Lecturer of the English language and Literature at Daejin Univ.
* Awarding: 1) The Order of Okjokeunjeong (August, 2010)
    2) The 24th the Main Literary Gold Prize of Heonanseolheon

Korea/조선형

심판자 앞에서

　따스한 봄기운이 일던 그 날로부터 앙상한 내 나신(裸身)에 걸칠 것을 찾습니다. 오래도록 기다렸습니다. 여름이 오면 에덴동산의 무화과 같은 넓적하고 커다란 잎으로 몸에 감출 수 있으니까요. 이제부턴 아무에게도 영영 발각되지 않을 거라는 생각으로 희희낙락 열심히 감추었습니다. 가을이 되어 내 안에 것들이 서서히 불안해 합니다. 감춘 것이 하나둘 드러날까 봐서 말입니다.
광장엔 삼삼오오 사람들이 몰려옵니다. 심판이 왔기 때문입니다.
바람,
햇볕,
물이 있었지만 진정한 심판자는 아니었습니다. 그것은
기다림뿐이었습니다.
늦가을 비 오는 날 나는 거리로 나와 항복할 수밖에 없었습니다.
"오, 주여! 난, 끝내 발가벗고 말았습니다!"

겨울은 거울과 같은 존재입니다.
나는 부끄러운 모습으로 그 앞 서 있습니다.

Korea / Choi In-kyung

The Voice of Essence

Love
followed by
pain and tears

How pure
that Love will be!

The bosom heaving
to embrace
the origin of Love
When closing eyes,
becomes
a star of fantasy
to bloom in the desert.

That Love opens
your heart and
a crescent moon
casts over the blue sea
a solitary's silent light.

Choi In-Kyung / Korea

* Ph.D.of Neuro Science
* Dr.of Counseling Psychotherapy
* The Spring of Joy, issued in 2023
* Winner of Kukmin Daily Spring Poetry contest in 2022
* Winner of 14th Kukje Poetry Contest in 2016
* Int'l Andre Marlo Association member(ADAGP)
* Founder, Korea Neuro Art Therapy Research Institute

Korea/최인경

본질의 목소리

고통과
눈물이 따르는
사랑
그 사랑
얼마나
순결하리오

그리움의
근원을 찾아가는
원초 품어 줄
사랑

그 사랑
두 눈을 감으면
환상의 별이 되어
사막에 꽃피우네

그 사랑
가슴 열어
청자 바다 위에
초승달
고독자의
침묵의 빛 되리

Korea/Choi Sun-ae

The Bean Pod on the Eyes

I want to make
The one-sided
Lover
Loving me atrociously
As it is the rude act.

On the day
When the bean pod is covered on my eyes,

The brilliant sun was coming up.

- Tr. by Won Eung-soon

Choi Sun-ae / Korea

* debut as a poet through *the Hanmaek Literature* on the recommendation of Park Jae-sam and Jo Yeong-hee
* now attending Jeil College (major: social welfare)
* former president of Suncheon Palma Literary Society
* director of the Suncheon Writers Association
* director of the Society of the World Poetry
* member of the Korean Writers Association
* collections of poems : *Nojim Mountain Pass (1995), A Song for My Mother, The Way to My Home Town, The Unrequited Love of Flower Buds, The Poet's Trumpet,* etc.

Korea/최순애

콩깍지

지독히 짝사랑 하는
님을
지독히 나를
짝사랑 하는 그대로
만들고 싶어

내 눈 콩깍지가 씌던 날

찬란한 태양 뜨고 있었어

Korea/Choung Kuy-cha

Scenery of the Lake

On the lake holding the shadows of mountains,
there's my mother's heart
wide open.

The ecstatic group dance of those migratory birds,
kicking up the water,
is also love and consideration
for precious souls of the family members.

In joy and sorrow, I remember
when we played in the water.
Fine rain drizzles, cleansing my heart,
on the rippling ripples.

Life, or living,
shines,
just like the scenery,
so beautiful and picturesque.

- translated by Woo Hyeong-sook

Choung Kuy-cha / Korea

* debuted as a poet through the magazine, *The Munyesarang*
* member of the Korean Writers Association
* member of the Millennium Literary Society
* collection of her poems: *Wake Up My Spirit, On the Path of Life* (co-authored), *Youth Burning in the Sunset* (co-authored)
* literary award: the Millennium Literary Award

Korea/정귀자

호반의 풍경

산 그림자 품고 있는 호반엔
어머니의 가슴이
넓게 드리워져 있고

물비늘 헤집는
저 철새들의 황홀한 군무(群舞)들 또한
사랑이고 배려이며
가족들의 귀한 혼령이다

그 속을 노닐던
우리들의 환희와 애환 속에
잔주름 일렁이는 물이랑에도
내 마음 씻기운 꽃비가 내린다

생명이고 삶이란
저리도 곱고 아름다운
한 폭의 그림 같은 풍광으로
빛을 이루고 있다

Korea/Chun Byung-ok

Yearning

In the early summer missing the way,
At the end of the empty sky on June
After the rain swept up refreshingly,

I fly out a little bird named 'meditation'
As if it is something to see.

Flap, flap,

It has been a long time since I saw you
The disgraces and insults of the many days!
Flashing across my mind hit upon
For the wet alley into my mind,

Come out quick,
For the new sky in the east of Eden
Shaking off the deep green dawn fog
Of its valley in the forest.

- Tr. by Won Eung-soon

Chun Byung-ok / Korea

* She debuted through the magazine, *the Earth Literature* in 2005.
* Member of the Korea Writers' Association og Korea, of the Global Writers' Meeting, of the Korea Race Literature, of the Yesarang Female Literature'
* Board member of the Society of the World Poetry
* Vice President of the Korea Race Literature.
* Poetical Anthology: *The Rose-colored Sunset*

Korea/천병옥

그리움

길 잃은 초여름
탐스레 비 한 자락 쓸고 간
유월의 비인 하늘 끝

보란 듯 한 마리 작은
명상의 새를 풀어 날린다

푸드득 푸드득

얼마 만인가
습진 내 마음속 한 골목길로
문득 희미하게 날아드는 그 숱한
날들의 오욕과 모멸들이여

어서 새벽 짙푸른
골안개 숲을 훌훌
털고 에덴의
동쪽 새 하늘로 달려 나오렴

Now I Understand

Now I understand
All the things in the world
Exist in that way

One seed
Very thin roots of a stem
Are very important

I suffered unspeakable hardships
Now I became aware of
That there are nothing
Precious and valuable

The pain of a dying seed
The thin roots writhe in agony
To absorb subterranean water

Now I understand
The regrettable grief of
Shedding bitter tears
In the young days of parents.

Chung Chan Woo / Korea

* Consultant member of Korea Writers Association
* Consultant member of International PEN Korea Headquarters
* Consultant member of Association of Moden Poets in Korea
* Literary Prizes : The Boowon Literature Prize, etc.
* Books : The Write Smile of My Soul, 10vols.

Korea/정찬우

이제야 알았다

세상의 모든 것들
그냥 그렇게 있는 줄만 알았다

한 톨의 씨앗
한 줄기의 실뿌리가
그리도 소중할 줄이야

산전수전 고난의 세월 겪고 나니
귀하고 소중하지 않는 것
하나도 없음을 이제야 알았다

죽어 가는 씨앗의 아픔도
척박한 땅 속에 묻혀 생명수를 퍼 올리기 위한
저 처참한 실뿌리들의 몸부림치는 모습도

어버이의
한 많은 청춘이 피눈물 나는 아픔인 줄
이제야 알았다

Korea/Chung Jee-hong

You, Pasqueflower

I'll go back now.
Not showing mercy to others, I've lived on mercy,
and now I'm going back.

O my lust that was called love!
Forgive me.
O my pride that was said to be a good deed!
Forgive me, too.
O my fake personality that was wrapped up in words!
Shameful soul, ask for forgiveness.

Steam rose from three meals for me every day.
Now you're like a pasqueflower of deep wrinkles.
Lilies, roses, magnolias, evening primroses, and so on

Chung Jee-hong / Korea

* born in South Kyungsang Province in 1958
* graduated from Kyunghee University
* member of the Korean Writers Association
* vice president of the Society of the World Poetry
* steering committee member of the Thought and Literature Society
* president of th Goeungeul Literary Society
* collection of poems: "Underlining on the Heaven's Speech"

Korea/정지홍

are just dreams of a spring day.
My wife, merciful pasqueflower, sets the table.
It's a very gracious time of confession.

O time of greed without mercy!
Bend your back, for the mercy I seek,
in front of my wife giving me braised anchovies.

- translated by Woo Hyeong-sook

Korea/Chung Jee-hong

할미꽃 당신

나 이제 돌아가리라
자비라곤 모른 채 자비만 받고 살다가
나 이제 돌아가노라.

사랑이라 부르던 욕정들아
나 용서하여라
선행이라 하였던 교만한 자아야
너도 나를 용서하여라
말로서 포장하였던 치장된 인격이여
부끄러운 영혼에 용서를 구하여라

삼시 세끼 밥상에 더운 김
골 깊은 주름에 늙은 할미꽃.
백합도 장미도 목련도 달맞이도……
봄날의 꿈이다 할미꽃 자비에는
할미꽃 아내의 긍휼한 밥상 앞
은혜로운 고해의 시간

Korea/정지홍

자비 없이 배 내민 탐욕의 시절아
내가 구하는 자비에 등을 굽혀라
굽은 등 멸치조림 권하는 아내 앞에

Wind

My heart trembles
It is stuffy with no vacancy
But wind penetrates deeply
It stirs the heart with soft waves;

A thousands of year old beech
Shocked by the strong wind
It makes faint sound like a breeze;

Beach pines play the sea waves
Trees on the hills
Hail in full choir
Wild grasses dance together
Along with the wind
Twisting lips with the wind.

Chung Youn Hee / Korea

*The Moonyeasalang for Annual Spring Literary Contest of a Prizewinner
*Member of Korea Writers Association, International PEN Korea Headquaters,
*Member of Society of Millenium Literature in Korea,
*Book : *The Fragrance of My Soul*
*Literay Prizes : The Millenium Literature Prize, Epipodo Literay Prize USA.

Korea/정윤희

바람

가슴이 흔들린다
꽉 메어진
비집고 들어갈 곳 없는 그곳에
바람은 깊숙이 파고들어
조용한 파문을 일으키고 있다

천년 묵은 느티나무 뿌리도
강풍에 멍이 들어
실바람 소리를 낸다

해송이 파도 음으로 연주를 하면
가파른 산속의 수목들은
휘파람 소리로 합창을 한다
민초에 묻혀 사는 들풀까지도
덩달아 춤을 춘다
입술을 비죽이는
바람 소리로

Parental Love

On a night of silence,
my maternal love rises vertically,
hovering above the gas fire for food.

After this night, my lovely children
wake up and have a little chat.

Though I'm in pain,
I sooth my achy back
to add my love into the thick meat soup pot.

No matter how much I give them, it's not enough.
I'm always fretting about my lovely kids, shiny stars.
Though I burn and burn my spirit for them,
I want to burn even more.
Along with an overflowing scent,
I'll inherit the flower garden of my love to them.

- translated by Woo Hyeong-sook

Go Aeng-ja / Korea

* debuted as a poet through the magazine, The Munyesarang
* collection of her poems: The Fable of the Snail Bride, On the Path of Life (co-authored), Youth Burning in the Sunset (co-authored)
* literary award: the Millennium Literary Award
* member of the Korean Writers Association
* member of the Millennium Literary Society

Korea/고앵자

천륜의 사랑

침묵이 익어 가는 야밤
천륜의 사랑은 수직 상승하여
가스 불 위에 맴돈다

이 밤이 밝으면 사랑둥이
조잘조잘 입술을 만나다

아프다고 삐그덕거린
허리를 달래며
진한 곰솥에 사랑 한 국자 소롯이 넣는다

주어도 주어도 모자란
가슴 아린 내 사랑 내 별들
태워도 태워도 더 태우고픈
내 영혼들
넘치는 향기 품어
사랑의 꽃동산 물려주고 가련다

Korea/Han Jung-won

When I Miss a Magpie

The white dress shirt
goes well with the black suit.

Sitting with a bow tie
on the tree by my window in the morning,
the bird often sings a song that I never know.

The song opens my ears,
opens my eyes,
opens my heart,
and lightens my body.

Every street
has people who have lost their time.
While wandering to look for the time.
their hair turns gray, falling out,
but they don't even know that.

Han Jung-won / Korea
* debuted as a poet in 1998 through the magazine, "The Literary Trend"
* graduated from Chung-Ang University Graduate School of Art
* board member of the Society of the World Poetry
* member of the Korean Writers Association
* received the 23rd Award of the Literary Trend
* collection of poems: "A Coffee Cup Takes Off Clothes"

Korea/한정원

Sometimes when I miss the bird,
I put a piece of bird food by the window
and whistle to invite it.

- translated by Woo Hyeong-sook

Korea/Han Jung-won

까치가 그리울 때

하얀 와이셔츠에
검은 정장이 잘 어울려

나비넥타이를 매고
나의 아침 창가 나뭇가지 위에서
알 수 없는 노래를 부르고 있으면

내 귀가 열리고
눈이 열리고
가슴이 열려
내 몸도 가벼워지지

거리마다
시간을 잃어버린 사람들이
시간을 찾으러 방황하는 사이
머리털이 하얗게 벗겨지는 줄도 모르고
시간을 나르고 있어

Korea/한정원

가끔 그 새가 그리워지면
까치밥 하나 창가에 걸어두고
휘파람을 불고 있지

Winter River

The sea of my heart;
the world has always looked cold in winter.

In the deep river beneath ice,
my breath seems to flow with the water.

How long will it take
to endure the pain of sprouting
on bare branches?

No matter how hard it tries,
the wide river will not be filled.
The tears of those who have ever left
do not dry up in the desolate winter river.

- translated by Woo Hyeong-sook

Han Man-kyoo / Korea

* pen name : Gaek-un
* born in Yangpyeong, Gyeonggi Province
* member of the Society of the World Poetry
* e-Mail : Kyoostk@naver.com

Korea/한만규

겨울 강

내 마음의 바다
겨울 속 세상은 늘 추워 보였다

얼음 속 깊은 내면의 강 속은
나의 숨결도 같이 흐르고 있으리

옷을 벗은 나뭇가지에
새살이 돋는 아픔을 견디기까지
얼마나 시간이 흘러가야 할까

채워도 채워도
채워지지 않는 넓디넓은 강
떠난 자의 눈물이
마르지 못하는 헐벗은 겨울 강

Korea/Han Taek-kyu

Chili Peppers

Under the sun
that's so warm,

young chili peppers
are growing up in green clothes.

One by one,
the chili peppers

start to change
into red clothes

and move out
soon.

Han Taek-kyu / Korea

* poet, essayist, children's author, sculptor, marathon mania
* debuted as a poet through the magazine "The Thoughts and Literature as One"
* member of the Korean Writers Association
* 9th and 10th president of the 'Hanumul' Literary Group
* collection of his poems: Han A-reum & Han Song-ee, etc.
* book: The Record Card of My Life, and one more
* collection of calligraphy in wood: Underlining the Words from Heaven
* literary award: the 37th Main Award of the World Poetry

Korea/한택규

I also get
dressed in red,

following
the friends.

- translated by Woo Hyeong-sook

고추

따뜻한
햇볕 아래

초록 옷 입고
자란다.

친구
하나 둘

빨간 옷
갈아입더니

이내
이사 간다.

나도 빨간 옷
갈아입고

Korea/한택규

친구
따라간다.

Korea/Hong Chun-pyo

Going Together

Following the light, following people,
you and I are the accompanying shadow.
Without the light and the sunlight,
the shadow would hide away.

Your heart is my shadow.
My heart is your shadow.
Along with the shadows,
we're going together even on a dark night.

Can each shadow of our hearts
also run off somewhere to hide?
You and I have one shadow.
So we'll stay together until the sun is gone.

Not changing forever,
not hiding for long,
we'll be together forever.
We'll be shadows to go together for a long time.

- translated by Woo Hyeong-sook

Hong Chun-pyo / Korea

* pen name : Cheong-myeong
* debuted through the magazine, "The Literature of Public Officials"
* board member of the Korean Writers Association
* member of International PEN - Korean Center
* former president of the Guro Writers Association
* collection of poems : "Mom in the Adobe House", etc.
* received the Korean Race Literature Award, etc.

Korea/홍춘표

동행

빛 따라 사람 따라~~~.
너와 나는 동행하는 그림자
빛과 햇볕 없으면
그림자는 숨어 버린다

당신의 마음은 나의 그림자
나의 마음은 당신의 그림자
우리는 그림자 마음으로
캄캄한 밤에도 동행하고 있다

마음의 그림자도
어디론가 숨어 버릴까?
당신과 나의 그림자는 하나
태양이 멸할 때까지 있으리

영원토록 변치 않고
오래도록 숨지 않고
영원토록 같이 갈 우리이다
오래도록 동행할 그림자이다.

Korea/Hong Yun-pyeo

Flowers Told me

Flowers on mountains and fields know the future,
giving off their sweet scent gently.
Flowers tell me.

"It's a great scent for posterity.
At sunset, people, so tired, frown and close their eyes,
losing their scents. But flowers are different."

You may fall down in despair while living in this world.
Sitting at the foot of a mountain with no good answers,
you just see the distant sea, not hearing sweet waves.
That is a message from flowers.

Buds come into flower brightly toward the morning.
Oh at last, the world full of colorful flowers!
With a promising future, with my eyes open,
I'll stand up to open the sky like the flowers.

- translated by Woo Hyeong-sook

Hong Yun-pyeo / Korea

* debuted in 1990 through two magazines, "The Literary World" and "The Sijo Literature"
* board member of International PEN-Korean Center
* advisory committee member of the Korean Writers Association
* member of the Korean Poets Association
* collection of poems: "Wintering", "A Red Rainbow", etc.
* collection of sijo poems: "Mother's Meal", "Last Love", etc.
* literary award: the Grand Award of Chungnam Literature

Korea/홍윤표

꽃은 내게 말했네

산하에 꽃은 미래를 알고 살기에
향기를 살랑살랑 내려 보내려나
꽃은 내게 말하네

그건 후세를 위한 위대한 향기라고
해 질 때면 시들한 얼굴 찡그리고 눈 감으며
향기 잃을 너와 내가 아니라는 걸

늘 허탈한 세상을 살다가 쓰러질지라도
화려한 담장이 아닌 산모롱이에 앉아
저기 먼 바다 바라봐도 향기로운
파도 소리는 안 들린다 꽃은 내게 말했네

아침을 향해 천하를 밝혀 색을 내는 꽃봉오리
세월을 익혀 자란 오색을 먹은 꽃들의 세계
그래도 먼 장래가 있으니 눈을 뜨고
꽃으로 하늘을 열어 가겠네

Korea/Hyung Jong-hee

Handbag

Looking at my heavy shopping basket,
my mother-in-law
anxiously rushed to greet me, saying,
"Mountains and fields go down people's throats."

When I received the small palm-sized bag
as a gift from her,

I snorted, thinking,
"Oh, my! When will I ever carry a bag like this?"
It feels like yesterday.

I usually wore a big bag
that's the size of a postman's bag
on my shoulder.
But now
Mother,
I'm carrying the light bag you gave me.

- translated by Woo Hyeong-sook

Hyung Jong-hee / Korea

* poetry reciter
* debuted as a poet through the magazine, "The Hanmaek Literature"
* member of the Korean Writers Association
* member of the Gangnam Writers Association
* board member of the Society of the World Poetry
* collection of her poems: "The Light of High Noon", etc.

Korea/형정희

손가방

"산도 들도 다 사람 목으로 넘어간단다"
며느리 무거운 장바구니를 걱정하시며
버선발로 마중 나오시던
시어머니

손바닥만 한 작은 가방을
선물 받던 날

치, 언제 이런 가방
들어 볼 일이 있을라구
코웃음 짓던 일 엊그제인데

우체부 아저씨 가방만 한
큰 가방만 어깨에 매던 제가
이제
그 가벼운 가방을
손에 들었습니다
어머니

Korea/Jang Dong-suck

Woman in Autumn

Every time I see the back of a woman
in dark red clothes,
emerald memories come back to me.

Leaves enjoyed the best life ever;
now a few last leaves on the tree,
just hugging faded colors of time,
struggle with deep longing.

With every mark left by the fall,
Aria's dream disappeared long ago;
there are only faint memories left.

Jang Dong-suck / Korea

* debuted as a poet through the monthly magazine, The Korean Poetry"
* president of the Guro branch of the Korean Federation of Arts and Culture
* 12th and 13th president of the Guro branch of the Korean Writers Association
* board member of the Word Poetry Society and the Korean Forest Literature Association
* collection of his poems: "Watercolor Painting for Guro-dong", "Poetry Written on the Water", "The Way Fallen Leaves Go", and twelve more
* literary award: the World Poetry Award (grand award), the Guro Literary Award, the Korean Creative Writing Award (grand award), etc.

Korea/장동석

One leaf and two leaves
reflected on the young dreams all night;
now they only outpour their longing
in the sorrow of dying soon.

Showing off the splendor,
starlight just falls down and sleep
on empty streets;
oh, the sad back of a woman sobbing silently.

Autumn leaves emerge from deep despair,
drifting about at the mercy of the wind
in search of another dream.

- translated by Woo Hyeong-sook

Korea/Jang Dong-suck

가을의 여인

검붉은 옷자락을 걸친
여인의 뒷모습을 볼 때마다
에메랄드빛 추억들이 되살아난다

최고 멋진 생애(生涯)를 살고
세월의 진부한 빛깔을 무심히 껴안은 채
진한 그리움에 몸부림치는
마지막 남은 잎새들

가을이 남기고 간 자국마다
아리아의 꿈은 사라진 지 오래됐고
아련한 추억들만 남아
한잎 두잎
초연의 꿈 조각들을 밤새 회상(回想)하다가
죽음을 맞이하는 설움에
그리움만 자꾸 토해 내고 있구나

화려함을 선보이고
텅 빈 거리마다
별빛도 무심코 잠이 들고
말없이 흐느끼는 여인의 슬픈 뒷모습뿐

Korea/장동석

깊은 절망(絶望)을 빠져 나와
바람 불면 부는 대로
또 다른 꿈을 찾아 길을 떠나간다

Korea/Jeong Ji-ahn

Living Like a Dream

They say, man lives for hundred years or thousand years
But is it easy to live a hundred years?
About the man,
Do live, with not being sorry to miss, truly not to be sorry.
About the love,
Do love, with not feeling the lack of it.
About the separation,
Do live, with not being sad to separate, truly not sad.
Then, is our life a dream?
Saying to us, don't do this, and that...
Such our span of life, short as long, and long as short,
And as unusual allurements of all sort are all lies,
Without being swayed by the process of mind and emotion
Rather, do live like a dream...
Forever, do live in a dream...

- Tr. by Won Eung-soon

Jeong Ji-ahn / Korea

* member of the Society of the World Poetry
* member of the Korean Writers Association
* member of the Korean center of International PEN
* collection of poems: *Half Past Five in the Morning*, and many more

Korea/정지안

꿈같이 사시도록

백년 천년 산다고는 하지만
백년 살기는 쉬운가요?
사람에 대해서
그리워하지 정말 그리워 말고 사시도록
사랑에 대해서
아쉬워하지 정말 아쉬워 말고 사시도록
이별에 대해서
서운해 하지 정말 서운해 말고 사시도록
그러면 삶이 꿈인가요?
이것도 말라 저것도 말라시면……
마음 작용, 감정 작용에 지배당하지 말고
짧은 듯 긴 또 긴 듯 짧은 참 꿈같은 인생
별별 유혹이든 뭐든 모두가 거짓부렁
차라리, 꿈같이 사시도록……
영원히, 꿈속에 사시도록……

Korea/Jeong Myeong-hee

Autumn, a Red Ivy

Like chili peppers spread out to dry in the sun,
ivy leaves embellish the wall in the sunlight.

The wall among the ivy leaves is like white letter paper;
In return for the warm sunshine,
the leaves write about emptiness like clouds.

The leaves shrivel up, getting empty;
the lonely ones, not making a way,
break into small pieces, one by one.

Is there a way for the leaves
to connect with each other?

Not connecting the way in autumn,
the ivy leaves have only dry thin stems.

Jeong Myeong-hee / Korea

* debuted as a poet through the magazine, The Literary Trend
* former president of the Suwon Writers Association
* president of the Gyeonggi Writers Association
* president of the Gyeonggi Forest Literature Association
* collection of her poems: *A Leaf of Love and a Leaf of Longing*

Korea/정명희

Red autumn seems to play cat's cradle with strings,
pulling the tentacles of the poor antennae.

A loose string that has not been let go;
late autumn gets a dream from empty fields.

- translated by Woo Hyeong-sook

Korea/Jeong Myeong-hee

가을은 붉은 담쟁이

고추를 널어놓듯 담벼락 장판 위에
햇빛을 불러와 바스락거리는 정겨움을 말린다

담쟁이 손가락 사이는 하얀 편지지
하늘 빛 눈인사에 화답하며 구름이듯
허허로움을 글로 쓴다

앙상한 슬픔은 여백의 잎맥
길을 만들지 못하는 외로움의 껍질은
한 잎 두 잎 부서지며 문장을 적신다

담쟁이와 담쟁이 사이에도
이음의 길이 있을까

다 내지 못한 가을날의 우수
뼈만 남은 담쟁이의 길

붉은 가을 얼기설기 실뜨기를 하며
가난한 더듬이의 촉수를 끌어 당겨본다

Korea/정명희

놓지 못한 헤설픈 끈
늦은 가을은 빈들로부터 꿈을 만지작거린다.

Dancing Island, Mu-ui-do

Passing through Jamjin Island, we darted to this island
which was united with Silmi Island, but is now divided.
Haegeumgang, a rocky cliff, is two kilometers away.
The fine sand beach on the island is covered in mist.
Bad pirates must have been withdrawn by an admiral.
Oh now it's a ballroom where heavenly girls have fun.

There are fishing nets off the coast far below my feet.
It is a good place where a lot of shrimp are caught.
No matter where we throw fishing lines into the sea,
we can catch rockfish, flatfish, and kelp greenling fish.
The seascape must be among its Eight Scenic Views.

Jeong Sook-ja / Korea

* pen name : In-hye
* debuted as a poet through the magazine, "The Hanwool Literature"
* graduated from the graduate school of service administration at Kyonggi University
* board member of the Society of the World Poetry
* board member of the Korean Federation of Culture and Arts Voters
* received a grand prize from The Lyrical Literature, etc.

Korea/정숙자

At the time when the tide goes down at low tide,
we walk across the sea to Silmido, with pants wet.
The West Sea is a great place to see the sunset.
Our ship, Muryong No. 5, sounding its boat horn,
plows through waves, and I think of fairy costumes.
The blue waves have been moving for a long time.
Oh the sea is really like my mother's open heart.

- translated by Woo Hyeong-sook

Korea/Jeong Sook-ja

춤추는 무의도(舞依島)

잠진도 지나 달려온 무의도
실미도와는 하나이다가 둘
오리길 기암절벽의 해금강
명사해변의 안개 낀 소묘는
해적 물리친 장군이었다가
천녀 노니는 무도회장

저만치 발아래 쳐놓은 주목망
새우 동백하 풍요롭던 터전
어느 곳에 던져도 물려 나오는
우럭 광어 놀래미 낚던 곳
무의바다 누리8경 길이나

한바탕 출렁이다 썰물 때면 때물리 지나
바짓부리 적시고 건너온 실미도
서해 바다 낙조의 도원
무룡5호는 뱃고동 소리 울리며

Korea/정숙자

항적(航跡)의 물꽃은 선녀의 매무새
굽이굽이 영영세세, 푸른 물결
저 바다는 내 어머니의 가슴이다.

Korea/Jin Sang-soon

The Sound of the Gate 3

The keeper of a thousand years of history gets a grueling,
but scholars become the spirits of heaven with self-interest,
so that every gate, big or small, looks so antsy.

Is the late-night street protest the only solution?
If there's no conflict or confrontation, it's peace.
No compromise between them makes us annoyed.

Green bamboos put their heads down in the wind;
chrysanthemums in frost are like lanterns at night.
The truth of nature solving problems. But humans?

Dirty paper money got us to live as water flows,
but we see the heartlessness of self-assertive persons.
The sound of the gate was a keeper for long in the wind.

- translated by Woo Hyeong-sook

Jin Sang-soon / Korea

* debuted through the magazine, "The Korean Poetry"
* collection of her poems: "Why the Wind Sits on the Tree", etc.
* literary award: the World Poetry Award, the Nonsan Literary Award, etc.
* vice president of the Society of the World Poetry
* former president of the Gimje Writers Association
* member of the Jeonbuk Writers Association

Korea/진상순

문소리·3

역사의 천년지기가 수난을 당하여도
선비는 하늘의 영이 되고 이기심만 야기되어
대문에 이어 싸리문까지 발싸심을 한다

야심한 밤 거리농성 그것만이 해결책인가
갈등과 대립이 아니라면 일련의 평화련만
타협의 양보 없으니 보는 맘 애간장 녹는다

청대는 바람 불면 고개를 숙이고
서릿발에 핀 국화는 호젓한 밤 등불 되어
숙어를 푸는 자연의 진리, 하물며 인간은 어떤가

때 묻은 지폐가 물같이 살라 했건만
무아경에 빠져서 비정의 실밥이 난무,
천추의 바람 속에서 수호신이 된 문소리

Korea/Ju Jung-hyun

News

Waiting for news from my loved one,
I feel thirsty and stuffy.
She didn't say she wouldn't come.
But the sound of stepping on the leaves.
Is it the sound of her footsteps
When the leaves fall,
I keep looking back,
thinking of news from her.

Waiting for news from my loved one,
I walk with my hands in my pockets.
She didn't say she wouldn't come.
When a cloud rises over the mountain,
Is it what she looks like?
When the wind haunts my ears,
I keep looking back,
feeling her hot lips.

- translated by Woo Hyeong-sook

Ju Jeong-hyeon (pen name: Seok-cheon) / Korea

* debuted through the magazine, "The Thoughts and Literature as One"
* collection of his poems: "New Songs", " A Poet Writes a Poem and Dreams"
* literary award: the World Poetry Award
* member of the Korean Writers Association.
* member of the Geumcheon Writers Association

Korea/주정현

소식

사랑하는 이의 소식을 기다리다
목마르고 답답하다
아니 온다는 말은 없었는데
낙엽 밟는 소리가
임의 발소리인가
나뭇잎 떨어질 때
임이 보낸 소식인가 하여
자꾸 뒤를 돌아본다

사랑하는 이의 소식을 기다리다
두 손 넣고 걸어본다
아니 온다는 말은 없었는데
재 너머에 구름이 떠오르면
임의 모습인가
바람이 귓가에 맴돌면
임의 뜨거운 입술인가 하여
자꾸 뒤를 돌아본다

Korea/Kang Hee-seok

Impossible to Live Alone

In March, early in spring,
30 eggs were hatched.
I gained 20 chicks
and raised them in a hen house.

When the chicks were about three months old,
they split into female and male chicks;
roosters began to rank among themselves.

There were ten roosters;
one of them was a little late in development.
By the way, the other nine attacked
the weak one mercilessly.
Alas, bullying in the chicken world, too!

They pecked only at his head; his cock's comb fell off.
He couldn't bear them, only to find a place to hide.

Kang Hee-Seok / Korea

* born in Gochang, north Jeolla Province
* served as a naval officer
* served for the Korean Air for 20 years
* cultural commentator of Gochang Country
* debut as a poet through *the Literary Movement & Trend*
* collection of poems: *I Killed a Cow, The Song for Homecoming*

Korea/강희석

He couldn't eat, because he was chased every day.
He couldn't walk well and just tried to run away.

I had no choice but to quarantine him
in an empty warehouse to save him.
Not getting attacked for half a month,
he drank water and ate all alone
and enjoyed his freedom. About a month later,
he gained a lot of weight and could run a little bit.

I was relieved. So, another 15 days later,
I'd let him live together with them in the room
where they were born at the same time.

But a few days before they lived together,
I opened the door to feed him in the morning
and found the weak poor thing was dead.

He must have had a hard time living alone.
The disease of solitude is fatal
to all living things, after all.

- translated by Woo Hyeong-sook

Korea/Kang Hee-seok

혼자서는 못살아

이른 봄 삼월에
달걀 30개를 부화시켜
병아리 20마리를 얻어
한 닭장에서 키웠다

3개월쯤 자라자 암수가 갈라지고
수탉들은 자기들끼리
서열을 만들기 시작했다

수탉은 열 마리나 되었는데
그 중 한 마리는 조금 발육이 늦었다
그런데 나머지 아홉 마리는 유독
그 힘 약한 한 마리를 무자비하게 공격했다
이지메, 닭들 세계에서도

머리만을 쪼아대니 벼슬이 떨어져 나가고
견딜 수 없어 쫓겨다니며 가리개만 있으면 숨었다
날마다 쫓기다 보니 먹이를 먹지 못해
그 놈은 잘 걷지도 못하고 도망만 다녔다

할 수 없이 나는 그 놈을 살리기 위해서
빈 창고에 격리 시켰다
놈은 한 보름 공격당하지 않고

Korea / 강희석

혼자서 모이 먹고 물 마시면서
자유를 만끽했다. 한 달쯤 되자
살도 많이 오르고 조금 달리기도 했다

나는 안심했다. 한 보름만 더 지나
한꺼번에 태어난 20명 동료들이 사는
그 방에 다시 합방을 시킬 작정이었다

그러나 합방을 며칠 앞두고
아침에 먹이를 주려고 창고 문을 열었더니
그 약한 불쌍한 놈은 죽어 있었다

혼자서는 못살아
고독이라는 병은 결국
모든 생명에게 치명적이야

The Peak Named Anhyeonsuk

A Mom's bosom
Embraced like the horse's saddle,

Every season the forest is dense
The mountain's birds enjoy peacefully,

A ferryman angling for the space of one day
And the Han river streams quietly.

The signal fire of the lighthouse
With blowing gently and softly
The fertile land of Yangcheon village
Is spreading the flavor of rice.

              - Tr. by Won Eung-soon

Kang Young-duk / Korea

* pen name : Yeon-bong
* member of the Korean Writers Association
* member of the Society of the World Poetry
* She debuted through the magazine, *The Literature 21*, in 1998.
* collection of poems: *The Channel of Time*, etc.

Korea/강영덕

안현석봉

말안장처럼 품어진
어미의 가슴

계절마다 수목은 울창하고
산새는 평화롭게 누리하고

하루의 여유를 낚는 뱃사공
한강의 물결도 잔잔히 흐르네

산들산들 무르익은
봉수대 불빛
기름진 양천의
구수한 밥 냄새 풍기고 있구나

Korea/Kim Chong-ki

At the Start of Each Season

Surviving the freezing cold, I write "Welcome Spring, Wishing for Good Luck"; then, a warm breeze blows from somewhere.

In the warm spring, bright pretty flowers are in full bloom, and then hot summer starts with flowers having a big smile.

Summer heat and tropical nights make us soaked in sweat, but autumn starts with the cool chill waking us up at dawn.

When fallen leaves pile up everywhere in fields and mountains, winter starts with snow; who can stop the violent north wind?

We have lived, actually realizing those signs of the sky; I'm grateful to the inherent traits! I really love the seasons.

- translated by Woo Hyeong-sook

Kim Chong-ki/Korea

* board member of the Society of the World Poetry
* debuted as a poet through the magazine, "The Christian Literature"
* collection of poems: "Please Open the Door", and twelve more
* literary award: the Youngrang Literary Award, and five more

Korea/김종기

계절의 입구마다

몹시도 추워 움츠려 살다가 입춘(立春)대길을 써서
붙인 날 어디선지 감도는 훈훈 풍풍(薰薰風風)이 인다

따뜻한 봄꽃들이 얄밉도록 만발해서 참 화사하더니
뜨거운 여름날의 꽃들마다 큼직하게 웃는 날 입하(立夏)

폭염과 열대야로 누구나 모조리 다 땀범벅이었는데
새벽잠을 설치게끔 하는 서늘한 한기는 입추(立秋)부터

낙엽이 산야 어디에서나 수북수북 쌓일 때가 되자
몰아치는 북풍을 누가 막겠느냐 눈 나라 입동(立冬)을

이와 같은 하늘의 조짐을 몸소 깨달아 느끼며 사는
인간에게 주신 성정이 고맙다! 전 계절(季節)이 진실로 좋다!

Korea/Kim Don-young

The Empty Ship

One shaking ship
Waiting the unpledged time
When we don't know
In the flowing time and tide,

Sometimes because of its remote antiquity
The tear's waves arise
Though the sore injury is washed off
Into the sweeping waves,
We cannot press down
The ardent yearning.

Today
The evening glow fills up the empty ship
The only song to sing together
Spins itself around our ears.

- Tr. by Won Eung-soon

Kim Don-young / Korea

* pen Name: Eunro.
* graduated from the Air and Correspondence College.
* member of the Korean Writers Association
* He debuted through the magazine, *The Literary Movement & Trend*
* collection of poems: *The Whisper of the Wind*, etc.
* literary award: the World Poetry Award

Korea/김돈영

빈 배

흐르는 세월 속에
언제일지 모를
그때를 기다리며
흔들리는 배 한 척

아득함에 때론
눈물의 파랑이 일고
휩쓸리는 물결에
아픈 상처 씻겨 보내도
그립다는 간절함은
억누를 길이 없네

오늘도
저녁노을은 빈 배를 채우고
함께 부를 노래만이
귓가를 맴돌 뿐이네

Korea/Kim Eui-shik

Gospel in the Garden of Life

The Garden of Life is full of colorful flowers.
For the Gospel to take roots, birds sing holy songs
echoing through the outstretched arms of trees.

Wanting to light up darkness like a beacon of hope,
we sowed seeds and took good care of them.
Soon the seeds sprouted for a brighter golden future.

The Garden of Life
bore fruit with love and truth.
So my dream rises above the horizon of the sea.
Right here in Sihanoukville,
I'm living a new life,
filled with grace, expecting divine love.

- translated by Woo Hyeong-sook

Kim Eui-shik / Korea

* missionary and professor of Life University, Cambodia
* visiting professor of Incheon National University
* debuted as a poet and an essayist through the magazine "The Literary Trend"
* member of the Korean Writers Association
* literary award: the Literary Award from the Korean Elders Literary Society
* collection of his poems: "Becoming the Root of a Dandelion", etc.

Korea/김의식

라이프동산에서의 복음

꽃들 색조로 수놓은 라이프동산
새들의 노래 음표로 가득 채운 복음 뿌리 내려
두 팔 벌린 나무들 메아리로 날개 친다.

희망의 불꽃, 어둠을 밝히는 등대 마음 밭에 뿌린 씨앗들
싹트고 가슴 열어 매만진 손길
더 밝은 미래를 황금빛으로 수놓는다.

사랑과 진리로 열매 맺는
라이프동산
바다의 수평선 위로 솟구치는 꿈
여기! 시하누크빌에서
새 생명 심어 변화된 삶,
은혜로 껴안아 받을 복 헤아린다.

A Wall

Is the wall
A division?

A protection?

The place
An ivy is blooming?

What is
The twelve gates?

Is the great joy
To appear over there?

Though having soaked
The pretty work in water

Kim Hye-sook / Korea

* member of the Jeonju City Council
* She received a Ph.D. degree at Jeonju University.
* She debuted through the magazine, *The Literary Movement & Trend*.
*a student of the Grodunte school, Dept. of Public Policy Planning, Ewha Univ.
* award: the Manifesto Award

Korea/김혜숙

And placed it
In the grassland,

The time
When I put you
In my mind
Is most beautiful.

- Tr. by Won Eung-soon

Korea/Kim Hye-sook

담

담은
구분인가

보호인가

담쟁이가
피어나는 곳인가

12개의 문은
무엇인가

너머에
나타날 환희이런가

고운 작품을 물에
담그어도 보았고

초원에 얹혀
보기도 했지만

Korea / 김혜숙

너를
내 마음에
담을 때가
가장 아름답구나

Korea/Kim Hyo-yeol

Stumbling Today

Writing hard
for 360 days,
I've waited for him.
I still suffer
from loneliness
deeply in my heart.

No matter how much I call him,
he doesn't answer.
No matter how much
I shout him out,
he won't come back...

A heavy twilight,
on the shadow of death,

is stumbling.

                - translated by Woo Hyeong-sook

Kim Hyo-yeol / Korea

* representative of Eulji Publishing Company
* publisher of *An Encyclopedia of the Korean Poetry*
* editor of the Society of the World Poetry
* Address : #603, 41 Yanghwajin-gil, Mapo-gu, Seoul, Korea
* e-mail : ejp4050@hanmail.net

Korea/김효열

비틀거리는 오늘

삼백예순날
원고지를 두들기며
기다려도
가슴 시린
외로움이
부글거린다

불러도 대답 없는
사람이지만
불러도 불러도
돌아오지 않을
사람이지만……

무거운 황혼이
죽음의 그림자 위에서

비틀거리고 있다

Korea/Kim Jae-myeoung

Concession

The tide slowly
takes over the sandy beach
little by little.

The waves that rise and fall constantly
rush to occupy the sandy beach
with a thunderous roar.

The sand castles that children built hard
are broken by the rushing waves;
people jump back, yielding
the sand beach to the waves.

- translated by Woo Hyeong-sook

Kim Jae-myeoung / Korea

* born in Dangjin, South Chungcheong Province
* member of the Society of the World Poetry
* pastor of Sin-kwang Methodist Church, in Cheonan City
* Address: No. 77-17, Yonggok-dong, Chunan City, Chungnan, Korea(in Sinkwang Methodist Church)
* e-mail : kjm1210@hanmail.net

Korea/김재명

내어 줌

밀물이 서서히
조금씩 조금씩
모래해변을 점령해 온다.

쉼 없이 일었다 지는 파도가
천둥소리 같은 괴성을 내며
포기하지 않고 모랫벌을 점령해 온다.

아이들이 애써 지은 모래성은
밀려온 파도에 부서지고
사람들은 폴짝폴짝 뒷걸음치며
파도에게 모랫벌을 내어 준다.

Korea/Kim Jeong-won

The Prison Where Socrates Was Imprisoned
- During My Trip to Greece -

I thought it was a place where a beast was once trapped.

Visiting Greece, once-brilliant, under the sky
that has forgotten its past, I saw a small ancient cave
on the corner of a small hill.

Next to the cave was an olive tree,
on guard for the lonely cell, dozing off.

The grass field in front of the prison was bright
with flowers as white as salt, reminding me of the tears
of his disciples who asked him to run away.

Kim Jeong-won / Korea

* board member of the Korean Female Writers Association
* She debuted through the magazine, *The Monthly Literature* in 1985.
* collection of poems: *The Place of Void*, etc.
* collection of poems in Korean-English translation: *The Alter Ego*, etc.
* literary awards: the Sowol Literary Award, etc.

Korea/김정원

Gaining wisdom for life,
the philosopher was determined to be martyred for truth.
I thought he'd come out of the loose wooden door soon,
leaving his hope behind in the cave.

Even if the world is old and civilized,
his words are in our hearts as torches for us.

- translated by Woo Hyeong-sook

Korea/Kim Jeong-won

소크라테스의 감옥
- 그리스 여행 중에서 -

옛날의 한 짐승이 갇혔던 곳인가 여겼다

한때 찬란했던 그리스, 어제를 잊어버린 하늘 아래
자그마한 둔덕 한 귀퉁이
아득한 시간이 지나간 작은 토굴을 봤네

그 토굴 옆엔 한 그루 올리브나무가 보초병인 양
적막한 감방을 지키며 조을고 있다

감방 앞 빈터 풀밭엔 도망을 권하던
수많은 제자들의 눈물인 양 소금꽃 같은
하얀 꽃들이 눈부시고,

生의 지혜를 낚으며
진리에 순교를 작정한 그 철학자
금시에 허술한 나무문 열고 나올 것만 같은~,
당신의 염원은 토굴 안에 잠자고

Korea/김정원

지구가 늙고 문명이 찬란해도
남기신 말씀은 횃불로 살아 있습니다.

Korea/Kim Jong-hee

About Death

People forget about death, living really hard.
However, in the end, looking back on the past,
we face death covered in dark blue waves
in front of our eyes right before death.
We want to avoid death out of fear, but there is no way.
It's impossible to avoid it, because the exit is blocked.
We're temporarily composed of the atoms and molecules
that are doomed to go back to cosmic dust,
and we'll slowly disappear through the corruption process.
Death only makes us disappear from this world.
Organic matters from the dust that makes up our body
need to go back to dust.
The atoms and molecules that will return to space
will fly over time into the vast universe,
where atoms will dance together.
We will find out through death
that we'll be there forever, dancing together,
and that we don't exist.

- translated by Woo Hyeong-sook

Kim Jong-hee / Korea

* born in Cheongju, Chungcheong Province
* debuted as a poet in 1982 through the magazine, "The Poetry Literature"
* graduated from Yonsei University Department of English
* received the Christian Literary Award, the Youngrang Literary Award, etc.
* collection of her poems: "Until the End of the World", "Stone in the Water", "Out of Time", "I Am Too Far Away", "Light and Darkness", etc.

Korea / 김종희

죽음에 대하여

사람들은 죽음을 잊고 열심히 살다가
결국은 과거를 회상하며
바로 코앞에서 검푸른 너울을 뒤집어쓴
죽음을 바라보게 된다.
두려워 피하고 싶지만 피할 길이 없다
앞도 뒤도 사방이 막혀 불가능하다
우리는 우리가 생겨난 우주 먼지로 되돌아가야 할
원자와 분자들의 일시적 배열에 불과함으로
서서히 부패과정을 통하여 죽을 수밖에 없다
죽음은 이 세상에서 사라지는 것일 뿐,
우리 몸을 이루고 있던 흙에서 온 유기물은
흙으로 돌아가고
우주 먼지로 되돌아가야 할 원자, 분자들은
시간을 초월한 저 광활한 우주,
원자들이 춤추는 우주로 날아가
함께 춤추며 영원히 존재한다는 것을
그리고 본래 내가 없다는 것을
죽음을 통해 알게 될 것이다

Korea/Kim Min-kyeong

I Am Also A Flower

The festival of the 'j' island
Growing restless with inviting the spring flowers

Is all covered with the poppy,
The queen Yang Kuei-fei of the fragrance.

The music flows
As happy as the lake
Together with a feast of the flowers.

The lovers grasping hands,
The children following
Their mother and father with hurried steps,

The windflowers in groups of two or three
Are delightful in the festival for the spring flowers.

Kim Min-kyeong / Korea

* pen name : Cheong-sol
* member of the Society of the World Poetry
* member of the Korean Writers Association
* She debuted through the magazine, *The Thoughts and Literature as One.*
* collection of poems: *The Autumn Lady Who Is Dreaming*, and three more

Korea/김민경

The canadensis flowers
Forming groups as shy as at one side
Are beautiful like the pure white bride
Taking with a lantern.

It is like the transformation
Of the windflower
As shy as to say

'I am also a flower!!
I am a flower, too~~~.'

- Tr. by Won Eung-soon

Korea/Kim Min-kyeong

나도 꽃

봄꽃 축제로 들떠 있는
J섬 축제장

향기의 여왕 화초 양귀비꽃
온 섬에 덮었다

꽃들의 향연에
호수 같은 음악이
흐르고

손을 잡은 연인
엄마 아빠 종종걸음으로
따라가는 아이

삼삼오오 할미꽃들
꽃 잔치에 즐겁다

한켠에 수줍은 듯
군락을 이룬 망초대꽃
순백의 신부처럼
청사초롱 어여쁘다

Korea/김민경

꽃이라고 말하기엔
수줍은 할미꽃들의
변신 같은

나도 꽃이야!!
나도 꽃이라고~~~

Korea/Kim Myung-ja

Moving to Heaven

It's a misty rain to meet me;
I cry at the longing for you.
Looking at distant mountains, I wail;
missing you a lot, I call you out loud.

The memories of what's left behind
remain incomplete.
Oh, people going alone!
Like dandelion puffs
flying up high
without any regrets about the world,
you moved to heaven.

Kim Myung-ja / Korea

* majored in Creative Writing at Busan Women's College
* graduated from Baekseok Theological University
* debuted as a poet through the magazine, "The Thought and Literature as One"
* 7th and 8th president of the Hanumul Literary Group
* present president of the 'Thought and Literature as One' Writers Society

Korea/김명자

In order to survive day by day,
you put a lot of effort into the hard life.
And you just whistled away
all relationships and memories.

But thankfully, you became a memory
for everyone you met in your life,
though you bid good-bye to all.

I thank everyone for being supporting actors
in order to get one person upright.
I thank God for having let him live in the world
as a main character, if not the actual.
My love, where are you going?
You keep running without a break.

- translated by Woo Hyeong-sook

Korea/Kim Myung-ja

천국으로 이사

희뿌연 비가 마중 나오고
아련한 그리움에 울고
먼 산을 보면 통곡
그리움에 목 놓아 불러보는 당신

남겨진 것들에 추억이
미완성인 채로
홀로 가는 인생들아
세사에 미련 두지 말고
헐 헐 민들레 홀씨처럼
날아 날아
천국으로 이사 간 당신

하루하루 살아내기 위해
수고하고 애쓰던 삶도
인과 관계 추억들일랑
휘파람 소리에 날려 보내고

지나간 날들에 감사
살면서 만난 모든 이들에게 추억으로
이런 저런 인연들 안녕 안녕

Korea/김명자

한 사람 바로 세우기 위해
조연으로 사용한 모든 이에 감사
주인공 아닌 주인공으로
세상 삶 주신 하나님 감사
쉼 없이 달려 달려
어디로 가시나요.

Korea/Kim Seong-un

My Family Photo

When I feel lonely
my family photo soothes my heart.

When a blizzard rages,
rattling the windows at night,
the photo is
a great comfort to me.
easing my loneliness.

Just hanging on the wall,
the photo guards my lonely room;
when my mind wanders,
it is a consolation to me.

The faded family photo
is my only treasure;
it's definitely a keeper
that protects my soul.

- translated by Woo Hyeong-sook

Kim Seong-un / Korea

* born in Mu-an, South Jeolla Province
* steering committee member of the 'Thoughts and Literature as One' Writers Society
* CEO of Samgwang
* collection of his poems: "The Scent of Paradise", "The Path of Spring", "A Bonfire"

Korea/김성운

가족사진

외로울 때면
내 마음을 달래준다

설한풍 몰아치고
창문 흔드는 밤
허전한 마음 달래주는
가족사진 한 장
위안으로 다가온다

외로이 벽에 걸려
고독한 방을 지키고
흔들리는 이 가슴
이 가슴을 위안으로 달랜다

색 바랜 가족사진
유일한 나의 보물
이 가슴 지키는
내 영혼의 파수꾼이다.

Korea/Kim Young-sun

A Man Drinking Happiness

He says he drinks happiness,
filling his glass with today; tomorrow is his side dish.
Getting deep dimples on his cheeks,
he talks and raises his wine glass.
Happiness, going down his throat, is on the seesaw.
Going through disinfection, the happiness is fresh,
like dipping sea squirts in chili-pepper paste with vinegar.
The dimples on his cheeks
look as hollow as his glass.
A man, eating a side dish of clams,
drinks happiness; the dimples near his mouth
also move busily and drink joy.
Before he knows it,
a bottle of happiness becomes empty.
Just as darkness drinks the sun,
the man with dimples on his cheeks
has drunk happiness and joy;
his heavenly day is passing by.

      - translated by Woo Hyeong-sook

Kim Young-sun / Korea

* debuted as a poet in 2010 through the magazine, "The Literary Trend"
* collection of her poems: "Time for Drunk Horses"
* literary award: the 37th Main Award of the World Poetry
* member of the Korean Writers Association
* member of the Seoul Poets Association
* representative of Nanum Music Hall

Korea/김영선

행복을 마시는 사내

행복을 마신다고 했다
잔 속에 오늘을 채우고 내일을 안주 삼아
볼우물 깊게 패인 사내가
두 볼로 말을 하며 술잔을 들어 올린다
목울대를 타고 넘는 행복이 시소를 탄다
소독이 된 행복은 신선하다
멍게를 초장에 찍어 먹는 것처럼 상큼하다
두 볼에 패인 보조개가
마시는 술잔같이 움푹 패여 있다
키조개 안주를 시켜 먹는 사내
행복을 마시는 입가의 볼우물도
바쁘게 움직이며 기쁨을 마신다
어느새
행복 한 병이 비워지고
어둠이 태양을 마시듯
행복과 기쁨을 마셔 버린
볼우물 사내의 천국 같은 하루가
지나고 있다

Korea/Ko Bang-kyu

Roses

With sharp spear-like thorns,
roses create their own protective walls
and embrace the scorching heat
with their whole body.

Oh such rapturous beauty as a crown,
and the charming pride.

As if throwing up blood,
roses are torn and show blood-like red marks
for passionate relationships.

I guess
they keep emotional pain inside,
perhaps as sharp as their thorns,
that they have to endure alone
in secret.

- translated by Woo Hyeong-sook

Ko Bang-kyu / Korea

* president of the New Age Literature Society/Masan branch
* investigator of the National History Compilation Committee
* director of the Society of the World Poetry
* vice president of the Gochang Writers Association
* collection of his poems : *The Whispering of the Lotus*, etc.
* literary award: Grand Prize of the World Poetry, etc.

Korea/고방규

장미

날카로운 창으로
무섭게
보호장벽 만들고
불볕 뜨거운 복더위 온몸에 안으며

왕관처럼 황홀한
아름다움 드러내는 매력적인 그 도도함

피 토하듯
정열적인 인연 피우기 위해
찢기우는 핏자국 그림들을 만들고

그처럼
깊은 마음속에 남몰래
삭여야 하는 속마음에
가시처럼 날카로운
아픈 사연이 있나 봅니다

Korea/Koo Myong-sook

Flower in the Movie

In the grassland,
I was with magpies, sparrows, and cats.
The side door of the world creaks open,
and I stay at the end of the grass for a while.

I feel like I'm floating on clouds;
then grass flowers stop me,
asking,
"Where is our love gone?"

Like a flower trapped in the screen,
my poem
can't come out of the door.
It's only my heart that forgives me.

Breathing out, clenching my toes,
I try to push the iron door open.

- translated by Woo Hyeong-sook

Koo Myong-sook / Korea

* professor emeritus at Sookmyung Women's University
* vice president of the Korean Female Writers Association
* debuted as a poet in 1999 through the magazine, "The Poetic Literature", and then in 2009 through the magazine, "The Poetry and Poetics"
* collection of her poems: "How Many Sacks of Rice Did She Wash and Cook to Bring Here?" etc.
* literary award: the 37th Grand Award of the World Poetry, etc.

Korea/구명숙

영화 속의 꽃

풀숲 나라에서
까치 참새 고양이를 만났다
세상 쪽문이 빼끗 열리고
나도 잠시 풀잎 끝에 머문다

구름 위를 둥둥 떠가는 발걸음
풀꽃들이 길을 막아서며
묻는다
우리 사랑은 어디로 갔는가?

화면 속에 갇혀 버린 꽃처럼
문밖으로 나오지 못하는
나의 시
그런 나를 용서하는 건 내 마음뿐

발끝까지 숨을 내쉬며
철문을 밀어본다

Korea/Kwon Young-e

I Walk Down a Forest Path with Happiness

When am I thankful?
It's when I realize
that the happiness that comes to me is not natural.
When I attach a meaning to everything,
I feel gratitude and happiness.
It's amazing to wake up from a deep sleep at dawn;
I'm thankful that I can breathe fresh air
and see the blue sky.

The glare of sunshine brings me a feeling of happiness.
This hot summer is gone and it is a cool autumn.
Fascinated by the trees of Gwanak Mountain nearby,
I go for a walk in the early morning.
Walking through the trees,, I boost my leg power.
Compared to the trees that will always stand there,
how happy and grateful I am!

Kwon Young-e / Korea

* pen name: Cheong-gye
* member of the Society of the World Poetry
* member of the Seocho Writers Association
* adviser of the Saehan Daily Newspaper

Korea/권영이

I feel proud that I have the soul
that the trees don't have.
Because I have a place in heaven
where my soul will be forever at peace,
I greet the happy Sunday dawn with gratitude.
"I seem to have nothing, but I have everything",
I shout confidently and comfortably.
"Hooray~"

                          - translated by Woo Hyeong-sook

Korea/Kwon Young-e

행복감으로 숲길을 걷다

감사한 마음은 언제 생길까
내게 오는 행복감이
당연한 것이 아님을 알고부터다
매사에 어떤 의미를 붙일 때
감사와 행복은 싹이 튼다
새벽 깊은 잠에서 깨어난 것도 놀라운 일이며
쨍한 공기를 마시고
파란 하늘을 볼 수 있음에 감사하다

눈부신 햇살에 행복감이 밀려온다
무덥던 올 여름도 가고 서늘한 가을이다
근처 관악산 숲에 이끌려 새벽산책을 나선다
빽빽한 나무 사이를 걸으며
튼실한 다리에 힘을 주며
늘 그 자리에 서 있을 나무들보다
나는 얼마나 행복하고 감사한 존재인가

나무들에게는 없을
내 영혼이 있음에 으쓱한 기분이다
내 영혼이 영원히 안주할
천국에 거처가 준비돼 있음에
"아무것도 없는 자 같으나 모든 것을 가진 자"답게
당당하고 안락한 마음으로

Korea/권영이

"야~호~"
소리치며 감사하고 행복한 주일 새벽을 깨운다

Korea/Lee Byung-seok

The Autumnal Equinox

The chirrup of the cicadas
The sultry weather
Passed away,

The autumn wind
Chirping cricket
Blows softly.

The abundant grains
On the open field
With their head down,

The cosmos flower
Along the path
Is delighted to see me.

- Tr. by Won Eung-soon

Lee Byung-seok / Korea

* Debut as a poet through *the Literary Movement and Trend*
* Received the World Poetry Award, Award of President of Korea
* Ph.D. in Management of Administration from Hannam University
* Board member of the Society of the World Poetry
* President of Samil Industry Co, Ltd.
* M&S Mentoring of Representative Director
* Joint Representative of Volunteering Service Union
* Collection of poems: *Emitting the Romantic Fragrance*

Korea/이병석

추분

매미 소리
찜통더위
사라지고

귀뚜리 우는
가을바람
솔솔 하네

풍성한
들녘 나락은
고개를 숙이고

길가에
코스모스는
나를 반기네

Korea/Lee Chang-soo

The Flower that Bloomed in Silence

Just like winter leaves and drifting clouds
in control of their own destiny,
darkness spreads into every part of our lives
as blood does.

Having so many things, years show all sorts of colors;
with the images created by solitude,
I, grey-haired, look back on my past days.
It might take a lifetime.

Night insects are crying with sadness
in moonlight pouring over the valley.
Alas, a bird on a thorn tree is trapped in its memory.

Lee Chang-soo / Korea

* debuted through the magazine, "The Joseon Literature"
* board member of International PEN-Korean Center
* board member of the Society of the World Poetry
* member of the Korean Writers Association
* honorary president of the Dongdaemun Writers Association
* editing director of the literary magazine, "The Wilderness"
* collection of poems: "The Island in Winter", etc.

Korea/이창수

All the memories of the past that don't set us free
still linger in our minds.
The most beautiful flower is the flower
that blooms even in anxiety,

not knowing
that winter is just around the corner.

                        - translated by Woo Hyeong-sook

Korea/Lee Chang-soo

침묵 속에 핀 꽃

겨울을 보내는 나뭇잎과 나를 달아나는 구름처럼
운명의 두루마리에
인간 삶의 곳곳에 어둠이 핏줄처럼
퍼져 있다

너무 많은 것을 다 먹어 치운 세월이 온갖 빛깔로 진동하고
고독이 배양시켰던 이미지들이
내 회고(懷古)의 백발을 누이는 데는
일생이 다 걸린다

밤 벌레 울음 계곡에 쏟아지는 달빛 속으로
슬픔 참견을 나선다
가시나무에 앉은 새 기억 속에 갇혀 있네

쉽게 우리를 놓아주지 않는 과거의 모든 침묵은
자기 안에 품고 있기 때문이다
가장 아름다운 꽃은 불안 속에 개화하는
꽃이다

Korea/이창수

겨울이 막살아 숨쉬는 것을 시작하겠다는 것을
모른 채

Korea/Lee Eui-young

I'm Living

The absolute being high in the sky
asked me to take a look at the world.
So I'm living.

Like a sprout sprouting in the drizzle,
like a chick that broke an egg to come out,
I'm living.

Like a boy whose heart beats, looking at the rainbow,
like a trout going through the strong waves,
I'm living.

Like a waterfall falling several meters away,
like old heavy cumbersome overclothes,
I'm living.

Lee Eui-young / Korea

* debuted through the magazine, "The Baekdusan Literature"
* board member of the Seocho Literary Society
* board member of the Society of the World Poetry
* guidance committee member of the New Literature Society
* collection of poems: "The Heart on the Road", "Rhapsody of a Grass Flower", etc.
* literary award: the Baekdusan Award, the Seocho Literary Award, etc.

Korea/이의영

Pushed by time, and driven by time,
not knowing the day I can meet Him
who resides high in the sky,
guessing tomorrow can be the day,
I'm living.

- translated by Woo Hyeong-sook

Korea/Lee Eui-young

사노라네

하늘 저 높은 곳에 계시는 분이
세상 구경 한번 해 보라 하시어
사노라네

보슬비 맞으며 돋아나는 새싹같이
알을 깨고 나온 병아리같이
사노라네

무지개를 보고 가슴 뛰는 소년같이
거센 물결을 헤쳐 오르는 송어같이
사노라네

수미터를 떨어져 내리는 폭포수같이
날 지난 무겁고 거추장스런 덧옷같이
사노라네

Korea/이의영

시간에 떠밀리고 세월에 이끌려 가며
하늘 저 높은 곳에 계시는
그분 만날 날이
언제일지 아니면 내일일지도 모르며
사노라네

Korea/Lee Gyu-ik

A Lotus Blossom

Raising my head quietly
Under the umbrella, the soft gutter at the eaves,
The lotus blossom is tuning the dyes,

The lotus blossom
Coming into bloom in pieces
And its petals shaping one by one ply,

Stand lightly
On the fallen waterdrops on leaves
Attracting all men's eyes.

- Tr. by Won Eung-soon

Lee Gyu-ik / Korea

* born in Wooljin, North Kyeongsang Province
* board member of the Society of the World Poetry
* debuted as a poet in 2004 through the magazine, "The Literary Movement & Trend"
* collection of poems: "A Fine Afternoon", etc.
* literary award: the World Poetry Award, etc.

Korea/이규익

연꽃

조용한 물받이 우산 속
살며시 고개 들어
물감 조율하며

조각조각 피어난 연꽃
한올 한올 빗어낸 꽃잎
모든 이의 눈빛을 당기고

물방울 굴러 떨어진
잎새 위에 살포시
서 있네

A Feast Made From Meditation

When silence fills in
Only the space of mine
A yearning comes to my mind

Theree is delicacy that made
The varieties of meditation soliloquizing becomes a language
Water colors and oil painting regenerate as oriental picture

Some times there are mountain birds
And streams of rivers
The bright moon embraces stars
And shakes me to wake up my soul

At that time
The silence of solitude as the moon of daytime
Becomes the wings of ecstasy
And flies high,
I imagine the only monologue of myself
To brandish this world.

Lee Han-hee / Korea

* The Ministry of Home of Affairs of the National Police Agency
* The Moonyeasalang for Annual Spring Literary Contest of a Prizewinner
* Member of Korea Writers Association
* Member of International PEN Korea Headquarters
* Member of the Society of Millenium Literature in Korea
* Member of the Society of Poet Literary Coterie in Korea
* Literary Prizes ; The Millenium Literature Prize
* Books ; *The Sculptures of My Soul*

Korea/이한희

사색으로 만든 향연

고요의 적막이
나만의 공간을 메울 때면
어김없이 찾아드는 그리움 하나

그 속엔 애잔함과 독백 어린 사색이
갖가지 형상화 된 언어가 되어
수채화로, 유화가 되었다가
한 폭의 동양화로 거듭나기도 한다

때로는 산새와 강줄기가 있고
환한 달 가슴이 별을 품고 앉아
내 영혼을 흔들어 깨운다

그럴 때면
쓸쓸함의 적막이
낮달 되어 빛나다
황홀의 날갯짓으로 세상을 휘젓는
나만의 독백을 그려 본다

Korea/Lee Ok-gyu

In Clusters

When the wind blows from the east,
  green grapes ripen in clusters.
When we live with a smile,
  our lives are filled with happiness.
When we walk 10,000 steps a day,
  we'll rejoice in good health.

Not getting sick but staying healthy
  is our wish in desperation.
When we feel so delighted,
  our lives are filled with peace of mind.
Good things come to us in clusters,
  when our worries go away.

- translated by Woo Hyeong-sook

Lee Ok-gyu / Korea

* debuted as a sijo poet in 2019 through the magazine, The Literary Age
* member of the Korean Writers Association
* member of the Korean Sijo Poets Association
* vice president of the Mapo Writers Association
* collection of poems: Shout in the Wilderness, Flowers Bloom in the Wilderness, In the Wilderness, Living Today, Sunset Is Beautiful

Korea/이옥규

주렁주렁

동풍에 청포도 주렁주렁 익어 가듯
웃다 보면 즐거움 행복이 주렁주렁
하루에 만보 걸으면 건강이 주렁주렁

아프지 않은 것이 우리의 바램이요
마음이 기쁘면 평안이 주렁주렁
근심이 물러가면은 좋은 일이 주렁주렁

Korea/Lee Pung-ho

I Meet Autumn

Since autumn comes,
the autumn that's already come into me faces loneliness.

Since fallen leaves roll in the wind,
the fallen leaves that have piled up inside me roll as well.

Since it's drizzling
in autumn,
the sadness that has stayed inside me
flows with tears.

Sharing lonesomeness, falling, rolling and dampness,
the autumn days
inside and outside me
are heading for the deep end.

                - translated by Woo Hyeong-sook

Lee Pung-ho / Korea

* He was born in Yesan City in 1958.
* He graduated from Korea University (Major: English).
* board member of the Society of the World Poetry
* former producer of KBS and SBS

Korea/이풍호

가을을 맞다

가을이 오니
내 안에 이미 온 가을이 쓸쓸함을 맞는다

낙엽이 바람에 구르니
내 안에 쌓였던 낙엽도 구른다

가을비가 추적추적
적시니
내 안에 머물던 척척함도
눈시울을 타고 흐른다.

내 안팎의 가을끼리
쓸쓸함, 떨어짐, 굴러다님, 척척함을
나누며 저 깊은 곳을
향해 걸어간다

Hokyongsanbang
- the House with Bright Windows

On the ground in my house
The falling leaves are covered
In one fold, two folds, and three folds.

The coverlets are covered
On the bared ground,

After the winter has passed
if the spring comes, the new life
Will be sprouted,

The lonesome heart of mine
Seems to be warm.

- Tr. by Won Eung-soon

Lee Yong-ho / Korea

* born in Jeonju, North Jeolla Province
* member of the Society of the World Poetry
* retired from POSCO
* rural Life at Jukzang, Pohang
* e-Mail: droppes@naver. com

Korea/이용호

호경산방
-창이 맑은 집

집안 빈 땅에
낙엽을 덮는다
한겹 두겹 세겹

헐벗은 땅에
이불을 덮는다

겨울이 지나고
봄이 오면 새 생명이
움을 틔우겠지

허전하던 내 가슴이
따스해지는 것 같다

Korea/ Lim Byeong-jeon

The Feast of the Bulgwang Stream

The glistening sunlight comes down
to the bank of the Bulgwang Stream;
the vegetation get dressed every season.
making the shrub filled with flowers.

White cirrus clouds often stayed
over each valley of Bukhan Mountain.
Now brooks from the valleys murmur down,
slowly winding its way
to the Bulgwang Stream.

Nesting near the stream,
wild birds hunt for good food.
Where are cranes?
Loaches cast a stealthy glance.

- translated by Woo Hyeong-sook

Lim Byeong-jeon / Korea

* debuted as a poet through the magazine, *The Earth Literature*
* collection of his poems: *The Stairway to Heaven*, etc.
* collection of his poems for children: *Those Who Live with Nature*, etc.
* literary award: the World Poetry Award, etc.
* member of the Korean Writers Association

Korea/임병전

불광천의 향연

눈부시게 반짝이는 햇볕
불광천 둔치에 내려와
초목들의 옷을 철철이 갈아입혀
꽃 덤불을 이루고

새털구름 머물던
북한산 골짜기 골짜기마다
졸졸졸 흘러나온 물줄기는
굽이굽이 흘러 흘러
불광천을 톺아보고

산새 들새 둥지 틀고
맛집 찾는 불광천에
두루미는 어디 갔나
미꾸리가 찾고 있다

Korea / Myung No-suk

On the End of October

Don't be in a rush.
Fallen leaves are leaving us
one by one.

Don't shed tears
at the rustle of fallen leaves.
October is going, but it will come again.

The wind sounds good when you're lonely.
But, listening to the gentle sound of the guitar,
have a cup of strong coffee.

Fascinated by the scent of coffee,
mountain birds may come to you.
Persimmon trees will make you happy, too

Myung No-suk / Korea

* pen name : Wolha
* born in the Isle of Sado that lies off the coast of Yeosu, South Jeolla Province
* member of the Society of the World Poetry
* former team leader of Samsung Life Insurance Co., Ltd.
* e-mail : mns1016@naver.com

Korea/명노석

When the sun shines, ride a bike;
when it rains, take a bus.
You'll feel good when you go out hand in hand.

Cosmos flowers
still in bloom by the road.
will beckon you.

The love that left you is gone
like fallen leaves rolling and going back into the dirt;
it never comes back.

Time goes by;
it may rain in the fall as much as your heart aches.
But flowers will bloom again one spring day.

You're having a hard time now, but cheer up!!

- translated by Woo Hyeong-sook

Korea / Myung No-suk

시월 그 끝자락에서

너무 재촉하지 마
낙엽은 우리 곁을
하나 둘 떠나가고 있어

바스락거리는
소리 들으며 눈물짓지 마
시월은 가고 또 오는 거야

쓸쓸할 땐 바람 소리도 좋으나
가만가만 울리는 기타 소리에
진한 커피 한잔 날려 봐

커피 향기에
산새들이 올지도 몰라
감나무도 기분 좋을 거야

햇살 반짝이면 자전거를 타고
비가 올 땐 버스를 타 봐
손잡고 나들이하면 따스할 거야

신작로엔
아직 코스모스
그대 오라 손짓하잖아

Korea/명노석

가 버린 사랑도
낙엽 되어 뒹굴고
흙 속으로 돌아가니 다신 오지 않아

세월은 가고
아픈 만큼 가을비 내리면
어느 봄날 꽃은 또 필 거야

힘들지~ 힘내!!

Korea/ Nam Chang-hee

The Hands of My Wife

My wife's face was pretty and a little fat,
But now she is very wrinkled
With having not kissing me once as it should
And the hands of my wife
Like the falling leaves,

On the path for twilight
The sun hangs in the western mountain
The cold winds are flowing down in her back
And so the colder mind holding more tightly
In afraid of losing the seized hands,

In any case the eternal destiny is not existed
If I seize her hands one more time
Promising the paradise,
They are still the warm, withered jujube tree.

- Tr. by Won Eung-soon

Nam Chang-hee / Korea

* Pen name: Inseok
* Vice president of the Society of the World Poetry
* Graduated from Suwon High School
* General Manager of Los Angeles Agency of Korea First Bank
* He graduated from Joong-Ang University.
* Prof, of National Far Eastern Univ. of Russia
* He debuted through the literary magazine, *The Christian Literature*.

Korea/남창희

아내 손

통통하고 곱기만 하더니
입맞춤 한번 제대로 못해 보고
쪼글쪼글 주름투성이다
칠십 넘어 팔십으로 달려가는
낙엽 같은 아내 손

황혼길
서산에 해 걸리고
찬바람이 등줄기 타고 흘러내리니
잡은 손 풀어질까 더 꼭 잡는
시린 마음

어차피 영원한 인연은 없다지만
천상을 약속하며
한 번 더 쥐어 보면
아직은 온기 있는 쭈그렁 대추

Korea/ No Jae-ho

A Chrysanthemum

Though all flowers
Wither even in autumn,

The yellow colored chrysanthemums in autumn
Stimulate by colors,

The chrysanthemums make our eyes bright
And make our head clear, our minds and bodies peaceful.

Your fragrance
Is novel to wait frost,

Your novel chastity
Is beautiful still more.

No Jae-ho / Korea

* The Welfare Study on the Aged, Graduate School, the Korea Univ.
* The Management Study, Graduate School, Jeunnam Univ.
* Director of the Taegochonglim Buddhist Univ.
* Chief of the Dongjin Chinese Medicine, Kwangju, Korea
* Chairman of the Dongbu Group, Korea.
* Member of the Society of the World Poetry

Korea/노재호

Why does the poet
Love the chrysanthemums?

Because they disregard frost,
Giving out their fragrance
Even in late autumn.

- Tr. by Won Eung-soon

Korea/ No Jae-ho

국화(菊花)

모든 꽃들은 가을을
당하여 시들지만

노란꽃 가을 국화는
색깔로 자극하며

눈을 밝게 머리를 맑게
심신을 편안케 하네

네 향기는 서리를
기다려서 새롭고

고상한 절개로
한층 더 아름답다

騷客[시인]은 어찌하여
국화를 사랑하는가

Korea/노재호

서리를 업신여기고
늦은 가을에 향기롭기
때문이다

Korea/Oh Jin-hwan

Forests

Through a pleasant and beneficial walk,
I feel grateful for nature.

Forests are good medicine and preventive medicine for us.
Forests give us mental comfort and keep us healthy.

Forests improve heart function and are good to lose weight.
Forests cure obesity and help us keep our weight down.

Forests have a mystery of creation and awaken us to beauty.
Forests are open to everyone.

Forests have various beautiful appearances every season,
allowing us to relax with a variety of colors and scents.

- translated by Woo Hyeong-sook

Oh Jin-hwan / Korea

* debuted as a poet in 2000 through the magazine, "The Literature 21"
* collection of his poems: "A Persimmon Left for Magpies", and three more
* literary award: the Tammi Literary Award, the Seocho Literary Award, the Arisu Literary Award, the Korean National Literary Award, etc
* former president of the Seocho Writers Association
* former president of the Society of the World Poetry
* board member of International PEN-Korean Center

Korea/오진환

숲

즐겁고 유익한 걷기를 통해
자연에 대한 감사함을 느낀다.

숲은 우리들의 보약이며 예방약이다.
숲은 영혼의 안식을 주고 건강을 지켜 주는 보금자리이다.

숲은 심장의 기능을 높여 주고 체중을 고쳐 주는 보금자리이다.
숲은 비만을 고쳐 주고 체중을 조절해 주는 명소이다

숲은 창조의 신비와 아름다움을 깨우쳐 주는 보금자리이다.
숲은 누구나 이용할 수 있다.

사계절 다양하고 아름다운 모습으로
형형색색의 색감과 숲의 향기가 가득히 편하게 쉴 수 있는 샘터이다.

Korea/Park Kyung-min

A Mountain Man And a Country Woman

There was a mountain man and a country woman.
The mountain man loved the mountain;
the country woman missed the sea.

The man climbed up the mountain;
the woman ran towards the sea.
Soaked in sweat,
he got a burst of energy.
In the breeze from the sea,
her hair was waving.

He and she climbed the mountain together one day.
He climbed up dancing merrily,
but she was huffing and puffing to keep up with him.
After climbing, the two came back down.

Park Kyung-min / Korea

* debuted as a poet in 2021 through the magazine, "The Thoughts and Literature as One"
* member of the Korean Writers Association
* member of the Kangbuk Writers Association
* member of the Nowon Writers Association
* published a collection of his essays, "Mom, Run"

Korea/박경민

She shouted, "Why do you climb? You come down again".
He answered, "I feel different when climbing up and down'.
She insisted it's the same mountain with no difference.
He said we couldn't know everything from one experience.

- translated by Woo Hyeong-sook

山 남자와 村 여자

산 남자와 촌 여자가 있었다
산 남자는 산을 사랑했고
촌 여자는 바다를 그리워했다

산 남자는 산을 향해 올랐고
촌 여자는 바다를 향해 달렸다
땀에 젖은 산 남자는
힘이 불끈 솟아 있었고
촌 여자는 바닷바람에
머리카락을 휘날렸다

산 남자와 촌 여자가 함께 산에 올랐다
산 남자는 덩실덩실 춤을 추며 올랐고
촌 여자는 씩씩거리며 올랐다
오르고 나니 되돌아 내려왔다

Korea/박경민

촌 여자는 내려올 산을 왜 오르냐며 쏴 붙였고
산 남자는 오를 때와 내려올 때가 다르다고 했다
촌 여잔 그 산이 그 산인데 뭐가 다르냐고 따졌고
산 남자는 한 번에 다 알 수는 없다고 했다.

Korea/Park Youn-ki

Oh, The Rose!

In front of you I,
Am a throbbing heart
Oh, the Rose!
Where is your heart?

Where did you hide
Into the root of the deep earth
Into the sharp thorn.
Or did you hide into the red pretty petals?

Are you even blushing with your mind
By confronting her steps
From the early dawn
With your red heart hiding at any place?

Oh Rose!
The rose blushing even her lips!
Today I eager to hear
Your throbbing heart close nearby.

- Tr. by Won Eung-soon

Park Youn-ki / Korea

* Graduated from Pacheon Primary School and Cheonsong High School. *Retired at SDI of Samsung(1999)
* First Debut as a Poet through *Literary Movement & Trend*
* Recorded as a Poet in "The Encyclopedia of Korean Poetry"
* A Member of the Association of Literary Movement & Trend.
* Vice President of the Society of the World Poetry
* Poetic Anthology : *The Twilight of Nakdong River*
* Won the Main Prize of the 31st the Society of the World Poetry

Korea/박윤기

장미여!

그대 앞에서 나는,
두근거리는 심장(心臟)인데
장미여!
그대 심장은 어디에 있는가?

깊은 땅 뿌리 속에
뾰족한 가시 속에
아니면
고운 꽃잎 속에 숨겨 두었는가.

붉은 심장 어디에 숨겨 두고
이른 새벽부터
마주한 발걸음에
마음마저 붉히는가.

장미여!
입술마저 붉힌 장미여!
오늘은 가까이서
그대의 심장소리 엿듣고 싶다.

Korea/Park Young-yul

Blades of Grass

Under the scorching sun,
blades of grass are wilting
and hang limply downward.
They look exhausted.

Just in time, a cool wind blows,
and the grasses greet it warmly.
Like gaining strength again,
they stand upright, looking fresh.

The exhausted grasses
are rising again.
It's the life of wild grasses.

Wild grasses are bound
to get back on their feet.

- translated by Woo Hyeong-sook

Park Young-yul / Korea

* president of the Society of the World Poetry
* publisher of the literary magazine, The Thoughts and Literature as One
* former president of the Mapo Writers Association
* collection of his poems: *Becoming a Stream of Wind*, etc.
* literary award: the Korean Poetry Award, the Mokyang Literary Award, etc.

Korea/박영률

풀잎

뜨거운 햇볕에
풀잎은 몸살을 앓으며
시들시들 축 처진다
지친 것이다

때마침 시원한 바람이 부니
풀잎은 반갑게 맞이하며
다시 힘을 얻어서
싱싱하게 일어선다

지쳤던 풀잎이
다시 일어나고 있다
민초의 삶이다

민초는 절대로
다시 일어선다.

Korea/Ryu Yong-ha

On the Way Spring Is Coming

When warm breezes from the hilltop,
bringing spring, flit through leafless trees,
green grasses start to stretch.
Waiting for a new day to come,
the grasses endured blizzard and frost.

Under ice sheets, maybe the last ones, in the valley,
a brook is murmuring down; oh the sound of spring!
At the end of winter, the water is singing in chorus,
melting down all the remaining ice there.

Wild grasses that hid in the fields over the mountain.
When the grasses come out to greet the new guest,
a haze is rising on the skirt of a woman
digging up spring herbs in the spring sun.

Ryu Yong-ha / Korea

* debuted as a poet through the magazine, "The Thought and Literature as One"
* member of the Korean Writers Association and the Mapo Writers Association
* literary award: the 5th literary award of the "Thought and Literature as One" Writers Society
* collection of his poems: "Mt. Sobaek by the Seocheon Stream", "Petals Fluttering in the Wind" and "Stories About Heaven, Land, and People"

Korea/류용하

Thanks to the dance of bees and butterflies,
all kinds of worries are forgotten;
I run and run just to hide myself
deep in the warm arms of my lover.

- translated by Woo Hyeong-sook

Korea/Ryu Yong-ha

봄이 오는 길목에서

언덕바지 훈풍이 몰고 온 봄기운
나목을 스칠 때
눈보라 찬 서리 심술에 숨죽여 새날
기다리던
산 풀 기지개 켜고

산골 마지막 남은 얼음장 밑 흐르는 물
봄 오는 소리
힘 모아 합창하며 한겨울 끝자락
신들리게 녹여 내고

산 너머 들판 숨어 있던 들풀 새 손님
맞아 들썩일 때
봄볕 타는 아낙 나물 캐는 치맛자락에도
아지랑이 피어오르고

Korea/류용하

벌 나비 춤사위에 세상 시름 얹혀
흩날리고
따사한 그 님 품속 뛰고 달리며
깊숙이 숨어든다.

Korea/Seo Keun-hee

Day By Day

Living
Is as beautiful as autumn leaves;
is it something to laugh about like flowers?

Deep into the night, it snows in large flakes;
the beautiful snowflakes
flutter down with tears
in the mystery of the universe.

I live in the same way as before,

Trees are not afraid of the night.
Suddenly yesterday the wind blew mischievously;
today the sun is bright, so I'm smiling.
Yes, I live in the same way as before.

If I keep living in the same way as before,
my body shall return to dust.
I'll go to bed with sincere prayer.

- translated by Woo Hyeong-sook

Seo Keun-hee / Korea
* debuted as a poet in 1989 through the magazine, *The Space of Literature*
* member of the Korean Writers Association
* board member of International PEN/Korean Center
* member of the Korean Female Writers Society
* literary awards: Heo-nan-seol-heon Literary Award, Seongnam Literary Award, Grand Prize of Korean Literature, etc.
* collections of her poems: *The Scroll of Time*, and six more.

Korea/서근희

하루하루

사는 것이
가을의 단풍처럼 아름답고
꽃처럼 웃기만 하겠습니까

함박눈 내리는 깊은 밤
우주 속 우주의 신비
스쳐 나온 아름다운 눈송이도
눈물 머금고 내립니다

그냥 그냥 살지요

나무들은 밤이 와도 두려워하지 않습니다
갑작스레 어제는 짓궂게 바람 불더니
오늘은 두터운 햇살이 좋아 웃습니다
그래 그냥 살지요

그냥 그냥 살다 보면
흙으로 돌아가는 몸
벌거벗은 기도 한 자락 깔고 잠드렵니다

Korea/Seong Nag-jung

Habits Are Acts

Every precious moment
leads to daily life unconsciously.
Everyday life is existence and space.

Continued daily life
becomes a habit,
and the habit is the result of acts.

Habits can change our lives like tonics for growth.
Repeated training to win medals for Olympians
and repeated drills of soldiers for emergencies, etc.
When those repeated actions lead to habits,
they'll brighten us to become the victors of our lives.

Seong Nag-jung / Korea

* born in Changnyeong, South Gyeongsang Province
* earned a master's degree in trade from Keukdong(Far East) University
* president of CK Group
* member of the Mapo Writers Association
* member of the Society of the World Poetry

Korea/성낙중

My habit
is with me suddenly one day.
If I act well and correctly to develop good habits,
it'll lead to health, harmony, and love.

I should reflect on why I exist
until I mark the last dot.
Then it will become a habit.

- translated by Woo Hyeong-sook

습관은 행동이다

소중한 순간순간
무의식 중에 일상으로 이어진다.
일상은 존재요, 공간이다.

꾸준히 이어지는 일상
습관이 되고,
습관은 행동으로 이어지는 결과물이다.

습관은 성장의 물약처럼 삶을 변화시키는 힘
올림픽 선수의 메달을 획득하기 위한 반복 훈련과
군인들의 유사시 대비를 위한 반복적인 행위 등
반복이 습관 되면, 강렬한 불꽃처럼
우리의 인생을 밝혀 주어 삶의 승리자가 될 것이다.

나의 습관
어느 날 문득 나와 함께하지만
좋은 습관을 기르도록 입지를 굳게,
바르게 행동하면 건강, 화목, 사랑으로 이어진다.

Korea/성낙중

마지막 점 하나 찍을 때까지
무엇을 위하여 존재하는가를
반추하면, 그게 습관이 될 것이다.

Korea / Shin Dong-myeong

Camellia in Winter

How gruesome! It's got such a terrible temper.
Like falling a thousand miles down a snow-covered cliff,
it fell straight down and ended its life.
Ah, blood stains.

Red-tongue camellia with a lot to say;
white-eye bird picking up the bird's stories;
when did the two promise to meet each other?

Ah spark of love,
you took your life
at the peak of your life.
Alas, an avowal of false love
caused you to die.

Your death, covered in blood, makes me sad.
I will comfort your soul, so when it's bright tonight,
please let go of your bitterness and rest in peace.

- translated by Woo Hyeong-sook

Shin Dong-myeong / Korea

* debuted as a poet through the magazine, The Literary 21
* member of International PEN/Korean center
* member of the Korean Female Writers Association
* member of the Korean Modern Poets Association
* literary award: Gaya Gold Crown of the World Poetry, etc.
* collection of her poems: The Will of Wings, etc.

Korea/신동명

겨울 동백

섬뜩하구나 매서운 결기가
하얗게 눈 쌓인 천 길 벼랑으로
단숨에 생을 요절내
붉게 물든 선혈

할 말 많은 붉은 혓바닥 동백
흩어진 사연 줍는 동박새여
언제 서로 만나기나 했었던가?

생의 절정에서
목숨까지 살라 먹은 그대는
사랑의 불꽃 화신
헛된 거짓 사랑맹세에
제 스스로 관(棺)이 된

피맺힌 생죽음일진대 애절타
영가 불러 위로하노니 천기 밝은
이 밤 절통함 굳이 잠재우시라

Korea / Shin Oh-beom

Jeongdongjin at the End of July

It is right that I should go if I come.
When I see you, it's the season when green grapes ripen.
The colors of the hot season remain on the fence;
the last week is passing by stairs.
You don't stop me from coming. You don't hold me back.
So I dip my jeans in the receding East Sea.
Isn't it great to see that no one is sorry for that?
The air conditioner is on;
the closed windows are rattled by the wind.
Even if it's hot or cold at Jeongdongjin beach,
I shake my leg under a sun shelter, tanning it.
Jeongdongjin Museum, winding like Vienna sausages,
is on the beach; anyway, time flows on the beach.
Only July is passing by. August is in the back car.
At the signal, the crossing is blocked with a whistle;
the car is sticking its head forward over yonder.
July, which will soon be forgotten, is almost gone.
After this week, my vacation is over;
I promise to see you again next year.

- translated by Woo Hyeong-sook

Shin Oh-beom / Korea

* won the 2019 Annual Literary Contest held by the Kukmin Ilbo
* debuted as a poet in 2020 through the magazine, 'The Sisamundan"
* member of the Korean Writers Association
* member of the Society of the World Poetry
* collection of his poems: "Underlining My Life"

Korea/신오범

7월 말의 정동진

오면 가는 게 이치라서
그대를 볼 때 청포도 익는 계절이라며
무덥게 느껴졌던 계절의 색깔만 울타리에 걸어둔 채
마지막 주쯤 계단을 지나가고 있네요
오는 것 막지 않고 가는 것 붙잡지 않는다고 해서
청바지 물 빠진 동해 바닷물에 담가놓습니다
아무도 아쉬워하지 않는 것을 보면
그리 반갑잖은가 에어컨 틀고 닫은 창문이
지나가는 바람에 덜컹합니다
정동진은 더워도 추워도
그늘막에 짝다리 흔들며 검게 타고 있습니다
비엔나소시지같이 구불구불 놓인 정동진 박물관이 해변에 누워 있고
모래시계는 사연을 아는지 모르는지 흐릅니다
7월만 가는 거지 8월이 뒤차 타고 온다는 신호가
건널목을 막아놓고 댕댕 소리치며
저쪽에 머리를 그리고 있습니다
어느덧 잊어버릴 등 돌린 7월
이번 주 지나고 나면 가고 없을 휴가처럼
그대를 내년에 또 볼 것을 약속합니다

Korea/Yang Hae-gwan

The of Truth Sound

In the silvery bright moon night
The sound a woman take off her clothes
Being heard from darkness,
It is the truthful sound
Keeping the parallel of the optimism,
Not the caricature as she pleases.

Come here my lover,
With your original mind,
Because when the dawn comes nearer,
I should wash out the dust of mind
Piled up in many folds
Having concealed into darkness of the deep night.

- Tr. by Won Eung-soon

Yang Hae-gwan / Korea

* pen name : Shinsan
* member of the Mapo Writers Association
* member of the Society of the World Poetry
* collection of poems : "If we Change the Korean National Flag like This", and three more.

Korea/양해관

진실의 소리

은빛 교교한 달밤
어둠 속에서 들려오는
여인의 옷 벗는 소리
이곳의 컷속 캐리커처가 아닌
옵티미즘의 평형을 유지하는
진실의 소리

임도 원초적인 마음으로 오소서
겹겹이 껴입은
마음의 더께를 벗기기 위해
깊은 밤 어둠에 절여 두었다가
동살이 진실을 앞세워 다가올 때
깨끗이 헹궈야 하리니

Korea/Yeun Kee-young

Facing Each Other And Loving

When I gaze at trees
in the mountains,

the trees are just standing,
facing each other,
even when I get closer to them.

Not showing
any jealousy at all
in love with each other,

they're standing
face to face in silence
toward the sky.

Yeun Kee-Young / Korea

* born in Jeungpyeong, North Chungcheong Province
* debuted as a poet in 2019 through the magazine, "The Journal of Literature"
* received a doctor of laws degree from Goettingen University in Germany
* former dean of Dongguk University College of Law
* former visiting professor of the University of Washington, Waseda University, and Goettingen University
* emeritus professor of Dongguk University

Korea/연기영

We'd better stand face to face, too.
Comforting each other,
let's walk together.

The sun
will shine forever
for our beautiful love.

- translated by Woo Hyeong-sook

마주보며 사랑하기

산에 가면
나무를 물끄러미 바라보면

가까이 다가가도
나무들은 그냥
서로를 마주보고 서 있네

아무런
시기질투도 없이
오직 서로를 사랑하며

묵묵히
하늘만 보고
서로를 마주보고 서 있네

우리도
마주보고
서로를 위로하며 걸어가세

Korea/연기영

태양도
아름다운 사랑을 위해
영원히 비춰 주네

Korea/Yoon Hyoung-soon

Rapture

Dreaming of a new birth
with irreversible rapture,
it was born as a flower.
Perhaps
it's because it has a lot of fears.

I can be hot on my own
but actually
I want someone.
Instead, it's a beautiful temptation
that comes to me brilliantly.
The reason is
that I have a lot of fears.

- translated by Woo Hyeong-sook

Yoon Hyoung-soon / Korea

* graduated from Jeonnam University
* won the poetry contest held by the Jeonnam Daily Newspaper in 1965
* member of the Society of the World Poetry
* literary award: World Poetry Award, etc.
* collection of his poems: *Nostalgia*, etc.

Korea/윤형순

황홀함

돌아갈 수 없는 황홀함으로
새로 태어날 꿈을 그리며
꽃으로 태어난 것은
어쩌면
겁이 많은 탓이다

혼자 뜨거워질 수 있는
진실 하나로
누군가를 애원하지만
눈부시게 다가서는 것은
아름다운 유혹
그것은
겁이 많은 탓이다

Korea/Yoon Jeong-in

The Way to the House of Dasan

The aroma of tea wafts with the rustle of reed leaves.

The path of the roots is silent.
Counting stone steps, I pass through West Annex.

Under the tall rock where intaglio has been preserved,
a camellia floats in the gourd of Yakcheon Spring.

In front of the old wooden porch, I bow to the portrait.
The taste of hot water for tea gets stuck in my molars.

A duck is sitting on faded fallen leaves;
Yeonji Falls knock on the pedestal rock of Mt. Seokga.

Pink zinnia flowers are dead silent;
birds are chirping merrily in the verdant valley.

Yoon Jeong-in / Korea

* born in Gangjin, South Jeolla Province
* debuted as a poet through the magazine, *The Writing Mountain Range*
* received the Grand Award of Poem and Culture
* board member of the Society of World Poetry
* operating director of the poetry group 'Poems Boom' in Gwangju
* CEO of Dasan Organic Rice, 'Clear Embryo Rice'
* collection of his poems: The Way to the House of Dasan

Korea/윤정인

The sun shines at the top of the Cheonil Gazebo,
washing every day in the water flowing into Gugang Port.

While making tea at sunset,
the aroma seeps into the roof tiles of the House;
daily deviations and laziness
are overcome by the words of Dasan.

- translated by Woo Hyeong-sook

Korea/Yoon Jeong-in

다산초당 가는 길

다향이 댓잎의 바스락거림에서 깨어난다

뿌리의 길에 적막이 깃들고
돌계단 하나씩 세며 서암을 지난다

음각의 정석을 지켜온 병풍바위를 내려오니
약천의 조롱박에는 동백잎 하나 떠 있다

세월에 뒤틀린 툇마루 앞에 서서 초상화에 묵례 올리니
다조의 물 익어 가는 맛이 어금니에 꽉 낀다

오리 한 마리가 바랜 낙엽을 깔고
연지 폭포가 석가산의 좌돌을 두드린다

백일홍 분홍빛은 죽은 듯이 고요한데
녹음에 젖은 골짜기는 새소리만 청량하다

천일각의 상투머리 잡고 햇빛 혼자 앉아서
구강포 흐르는 물에 속가슴 날마다 씻어 보낸다

Korea/윤정인

노을로 차를 끓이니
곡우차 향이 초당의 기왓장 속으로 들어가고
일상의 일탈과 게으름은
다산 선생님의 말씀으로 모두 녹아내린다

Korea/Yoon Yoon-guan

Talus

The rocky Islet, facing
the wild waves of the East Sea,
has a craggy cliff edge with stony slopes.

The torn black stones rub against each other,
rolling around, and getting smaller.
The black stones with holes say nothing.

Oh, I'll put a handful of soil,
so warm like my mom's heart,
under the large evergreen pine trees
that grow with honeysuckles and hare's ear plants.
Yellowhammer birds and wagtail birds will like it.

Yoon Yoon-guan / Korea

* debuted as a poet through the magazine, The Cheongil Literature
* debuted as a children's writer through the magazine, The Thoughts and Literature as One
* representative of the DMZ Literature
* executive director of the Christian Writers Association
* collection of his poems: *Peace of a Handful of Salt, A Trip with a Place to Stay*
* children's book: *Charles' Tomato*

Korea/윤윤근

The taluses dream like that again today
on Dokdo, the sad but fresh green island,
where waves come from distant seas to rest.

 * talus : a sloping mass of rock fragments at the foot of a cliff or a mountain.
 * stony slope : a slope where lots of stones are scattered.
      There are talus slopes at the foot of the West Islet of Dokdo.

- translated by Woo Hyeong-sook

Korea/Yoon Yoon-guan

애추

동해의 거센 파도
홀로 맞아들인 바위섬 자락
널 퍼진 너덜로 까칠하다

찢어진 검은 가슴끼리
비비며 구르다 오그라든
구멍 난 검은 입들은 말이 없다

괴불나무도 섬시호도 붙어 사는
넓은 잎 사철 곰솔 밑에
노랑턱맷새 알락할미새가 쪼는
어머니의 가슴 같은
따뜻한 흙 한 줌 내어주리라

Korea/윤윤근

기어코 먼 바다도 쉬고 가는
서글퍼도 싱그럽게 푸른 땅
독도의 애추는 오늘도 꿈꾼다.

* 애추(崖錐) : 낭떠러지 밑이나 산기슭에 암석조각이 굴러 떨어져 생긴 퇴적물
* 너덜 : 돌이 많이 흩어져 깔려 있는 비탈. 독도 서도 자락엔 애추 너덜이 있다.

The Bulguksa Temple

The way for a wayfarer
Along the mountain path
That has many thousands of way,

The ever green old pine trees
With the gnarled canes
On every branch.

It's the old city
Of Kyongju,
The Seorabeol land,

The bell sound of the Bulguksa Temple
That has circled round the hillside
Along together the rumbling of the mountain.

Let's listen to
The wave of bell's sound
Stopping our steps.

- Tr. by Won Eung-soon

Yun Ja / Korea

* board member of the Society of the World Poetry
* She debuted through the magazine, *The Daseon Literature*.
* collection of poems: *I Write Poems As If Sowing Flower Seeds*, etc.
* award: the grand prize in the poetry contest to commemorate the March 1st Independence Movement and the 100th anniversary of the Provisional Government of Korea

Korea/윤 자

불국사

산길 따라
나그넷길
천 길 만 갈래 길

가지마다
옹이 지팡이
늘 푸른 노송

천 년 고도
서라벌 땅
경주라오

산허리 감아 도는
산울림 따라
불국사 종소리

걸음을 멈추고
종소리 파동에
귀 기울여 보자

First Love

I have memories of red apples, the fruit of love, in my heart. At the end of the fall that year, when the cold wind blew dreary through the empty fields, my first love began as Cupid's arrow stuck in my heart. It was when red apples were waiting for someone to secretly pick in the autumn sun that he began to feel love for me. Putting red apples in front of me, he said, "They are for you". The apples spread their magic wings and were embedded one by one in my mind, digging a deep well and raising up countless truths like spring water.

- translated by Woo Hyeong-sook

Yun Su-a / Korea

* debuted as a poet through the magazine, The Earth Literature
* secretary general of the Society of the World Poetry
* president of the Guro Writers Association
* collection of her poems: *How Much do I Pay for the Poem*? etc.
* literary award: the 8th Guro Literary Award

Korea/윤수아

첫사랑

내 가슴속엔 사랑의 열매, 빨간 능금의 추억이 있다. 텅 빈 들녘으로 찬바람이 스산하게 불어오던 그 해 가을의 끝에서부터 큐피트의 화살처럼 나의 심장에 내리꽂히던 첫사랑의 시작, 그가 나에게 사랑을 느끼기 시작한 것은 자홍(紫紅)빛 능금이 가을햇살에 매달려 서리*를 기다리고 있던 그때부터였다. 널 위해 준비했노라고 내 앞에 쏟아 놓던 빨간 능금알은 마력의 날개를 펴고 내 안에 알알이 들어와 박혀 깊은 우물을 파고 샘물 같은 진실을 수없이 길어 올린다.

*서리 : 떼 지어 남의 것을 훔쳐 먹는 장난

U.S.A. / Grace Lymm

The Bench by the Willamette River

The warm sun touches
a bench
on the path
by the Willamette River.

An 80-year-old loving couple once sat
on the bench for a rest, and talked long,
like unwinding a skein of thread.
Their old stories were stacked one upon the other;
Leaving their warm body temperature, they left it.

The elderly couple came last year;
they are here this year, too.
They will come next year,
so the traces of their life
add more weight.

Grace Lymm / U. S. A.

* member of the Oregon Writers Society
* lifetime member of the Rhee Syng-man Memorial Society
* director of the Korea War Memorial Foundation of Oregon (KWMFO)
* former president of the Korean Society of Oregon
* literary award: the Root Literary Award of the Northwest in the USA
* collection of her poems: Beautiful Companionship

U.S.A. / Grace Lymm

Nostalgia for their home land;
the passion of life in their youth;
the achievement of their brilliant American dream;
the cuteness and growth of their grandchildren,
the symbol of their satisfactory life.

The quiet conversation
between the couple
is as sweet as the sound of a viola,
fluttering down on the ripples
of the Willamette River
which flows calmly around the bench
in the sunshine.

- translated by Woo Hyeong-sook

U.S.A./Grace Lymm

윌라멧 강변의 벤치

윌라멧 강변 오솔 길목에
다소곳이 놓여 있는
벤치 하나
따뜻한 햇볕이 어루만진다

팔십의 노부부 다정하게
쉬어간 자리
실타래처럼 풀어 놓는 옛이야기
차곡차곡 쌓아 놓고
따뜻한 체온 남기고 떠난 그 자리

지난해에도 왔었고
올해에도 오고
내년에도 와야 할 그 자리에
노부부의 삶의 자취가
무게를 더해 간다

고향 그리운 향수가
젊은 시절 삶의 열정이
화려했던 아메리칸드림의 성취가
만족한 삶의 표증(表證)인
손자들의 재롱과 성장하는 모습이

U.S.A./Grace Lymm

조곤조곤 나누는
노부부의 대화가
비올라 연주하듯 감미롭게
벤치를 휘감아 돌며
잔잔히 흐르는 월라멧 강물 결에
빤짝이는 햇살을 안고
살포시 내려앉는다

Watermelon Eyes

Uncork the bottle
and pour forth
carbonated laughter
into crystal glasses.
Slow rhythmic beating of drums,
a chanting flute
and liquid whispers,
dripping like melting wax
on the candle between them,
discussing social security
and the adverse effects
of Vitamin E,
while fingers encircle
on stalking hands
and feet bound
in leather and wood
tap to the beat of the drums,
flaming candle reflected
off glazed canines
exposed in chiseled smiles.
Cafe Mocha for dessert
and red rimmed watermelon eyes
that would melt
with any warmth.

Jeanne Leigh Schuler / U.S.A.

94 Santa Maria Drive
Novato, California 94947,
U.S.A.

U.S.A./Jeanne Leigh Schuler

수박의 씨들

병의 마개를 뽑아
크리스탈 유리잔에
탄산가스가 있는 웃음을
부어라.
느리게 음악적으로
두들기는 북소리.
노래하는 플루트.
양초의 떨어지는
밀납방울처럼
사회의 안전과 비타민 E의
반작용에 대해
토론하는 부드러운 속삭임
손가락이 다가오는
손을 둘러싸고
가죽과 나무에 묶인
발이 북을 치고 있을 때,
타는 양초는 뚜렷한 미소 속에 드러난
윤이 나는 송곳니를 반영했다.
후식을 위한 Cafe Mocha
그리고 따스함과 함께 녹으려 하는
붉은 테를 두른
수박의 눈.

U.S.A./Lenore Cooper Clark

Check Point

This is the summer of my fortieth year.
Not many things have happened as I planned
When I was making plans in childhood, clear,
For future things I wanted, small and grand.
The silver bird flies high; I soar aloft.
At home await the arms of one I love;
I snuggle back into my seat, and watch
The city's lights recede, from high above.

How strange, the dreams we dream in early youth!
In some oblique way, most of them come true...
But out of context, out of time— in truth.
The world we find is not the world we knew.

Considering my life through this past spring,
I'm curious what the next decades will bring.

Lenore Cooper Clark / U.S.A.

3828 Dexter Avenue
Fort Worth, Texas 76107
United States of America

U.S.A./Lenore Cooper Clark

인생의 점검

이것은 나의 사십 년째 여름이다.
명백히 내가 어릴 때 계획했던,
미래를 위해 내가 원했던 크고 작은 일들이
내가 원했던 것처럼 일어났다.
은빛의 새가 하늘 높이 오르고 나도 높이 올랐다.
집에선 내가 사랑하는 사람의 팔이 기다린다.
나는 내 자리에 앉아
그 도시의 빛이 공중으로부터 멀어져감을 본다.

얼마나 신기한가, 젊은 시절의 꿈들이란!
약간 희미한 방법으로, 그들은 진실로 오게 된다……
그러나 현실을 벗어나, 시간을 벗어나,
사실 우리가 발견하는 세상은 우리가 아는 세상이 아니다.

이 과거의 봄을 통해 나의 삶을 생각하며
나는 앞으로 10년이 무엇을 가져올 것인가 궁금해 한다.

U.S.A. / Park In-ae

The Traffic Light on the Floor

A painter in fluorescent clothes
draws a line
in a pious pose.

Not protected by anyone,
the man looks shabby,
but he draws for someone's safety.
In front of a supermarket, as tall as a castle,
he's kneeling down to draw boundaries.

   Day laborer, painter, yellow traffic light, straight line, LEDs, visibility, sidewalk and driveway, breadwinner, daily wage, working for survival, biting wind, concrete floor, cool air, street painter, childhood dream, life and death, life-sustaining, hamster on a wheel; alas, a life without exit.

Park In-ae / U. S. A.

* debuted as a poet through the magazine, "The Literary Trend"
* 5th president of the Korean-American Writers Society in Dallas
* head of the Texas Branch of the Korean Deca-Poets Association
* head of the Overseas Literature Development Committee of the Korean Writers Association
* literary award: the Korean Literary Award for Overseas Writers, the World Poetry Award, the Jeong Ji-yong Literary Award for Overseas Writers, etc.
* collection of her poems: "Horses Swallow Words, Words draw Horses", etc.

U.S.A./Park In-ae

Where he earned a day's worth of food,
dotted lines are left like ellipsis symbols.
Thousands of words, not gone,
come on as lights all at once.

The trace out of the boundaries breaks my heart.

- translated by Woo Hyeong-sook

U.S.A./Park In-ae

바닥 신호등

형광색 옷을 입은 화가가
경건한 자세로
선을 긋는다

아무도 지켜 주지 않는
남루한 생이
누군가의 안전을 그린다
성처럼 높은 마트 앞에서
무릎 꿇고 가르는 경계

   일용직페인트공노란색신호등직선LED시야확보인도와차도밥벌이일당목구멍이포도청칼바람콘크리트바닥냉기거리의화가유년의꿈삶과죽음연명다람쥐쳇바퀴출구없는삶

하루치 밥을 벌고 간 자리에
남겨진 말줄임표
채 삭지 않은 수천의 언어가
일제히 불을 켠다

경계를 비껴 간 흔적이 아프다

Winners of the World Poetry Awards

Year	Country	Winners
1986	KOREA	KIM IL-RO
1987	KOREA	LEE HAN-HO
〃	U.S.A.	ROSEMARY C. WILKINSON
1988	U.S.A.	VICTORY OURINE
〃	KOREA	MOON DEOK-SOO
〃	C.I.S.(RUSSIA)	DOLMA TOVSKY EUGINE
〃	ESPANA	TOMAS BEVIA ARANDA
〃	INDIA	D.K.JOY
1989	KOREA	SHIN DONG-JIP
〃	U.S.A.	ELLIS OVESEN
〃	YUGO(Sarajevo)	DR. AJSA ZAHIROVIC
〃	KOREA	JEONG KI-SEOK
1990	U.S.A.	DR. MARY J. BANERS
〃	KOREA	DR. KIM DONG-NI
〃	KOREA	DR. YUN JONG-HYOK
1991	JAPAN	UEMOTO MASAO
〃	KOREA	LIM JI-HYUN
〃	AUSTRALIA	JOY BEAUDETTE CRIPS
〃	KOREA	LIM HEON-DO

Year	Country	Winners
1992	KOREA	BAEK HAN-YI
//	BRAZIL	ANGELA MARIA ROCHA BIASE
//	KOREA	YANG SANG-WOOK
//	CHINA P.R.	CHEN-HUI JIN
1993	KOREA	KIM JI-HYANG
//	ISRAEL	ADA AHARONI
//	JAPAN	JUNKO HAMAE
//	KOREA	DR. KIM JOUNG-WOONG
//	CHINA P.R.	Prof. LU JIN
1994	KOREA	CHOI YUN-YOUNG
1995	KOREA	LEE CHANG-HWAN
1996	KOREA	SON KI-SUB
1997	KOREA	KIM MIN-SEONG
1998	KOREA	KIM NAM-WOONG
//	KOREA	KIM CHUI-KYONG
1999	KOREA	LEE JAE-HYUN
//	KOREA	JUNG SOON-YOUNG
//	KOREA	PARK KEUN-HOO
2000	KOREA	JIN EUL-JU
//	CHINA	GE NAI FU
2001	KOREA	LEE KI-BAN

Year	Country	Winners
2002	JAPAN	JUN UENO
2003	KOREA	KIM CHANG-JIK
〃	KOREA	KIM JI-WON
2004	JAPAN	NATIKO WATANABE
〃	KOREA	CHUNG OK-IN
2005	KOREA	SEO JEONG-NAM
〃	KOREA	LEE JI-YOUNG
〃	KOREA	JUNG U-HA
2006	KOREA	OH MIN-PHIL
〃	KOREA	KIM SUNG-YOUL
〃	KOREA	LEE JONG-IL
2007	KOREA	SHIN SOON-AE
〃	KOREA	CHO KI-HYUN
2008	KOREA	CHOI SEUNG-BEOM
〃	KOREA	KANG HAE-KUN
2009	KOREA	SHIN DONG-MYEONG
〃	KOREA	KIM JONG-WON
2010	KOREA	PARK MOON-JAE
〃	KOREA	LIM WON-SIK
〃	KOREA	EUN YO-SUK
2011	KOREA	KIM KYE-YOON
〃	KOREA	KIM IL-RYE

Year	Country	Winners
2012	KOREA	CHONG SONG-JON
〃	KOREA	JIN SANG-SOON
〃	KOREA	NO JUNG-AI
2013	KOREA	JUN DUK-KI
〃	KOREA	JUNG SUN-JA
〃	KOREA	OH JIN-HWAN
〃	KOREA	KOU SUN-JA
2014	KOREA	KIM KYEONG-SOON
〃	KOREA	KIM DON-YOUNG
〃	KOREA	LEE JAE-HO
〃	KOREA	LEE SEOK-GI
2015	KOREA	KO BANG-KYU
〃	KOREA	PARK IN-AE
〃	KOREA	LEE BYUNG-SEOK
〃	KOREA	WEE MAENG-RYANG
2016	KOREA	JANG DONG-SUCK
〃	KOREA	BANG JUNG-SUN
〃	KOREA	LEE SU-JEONG
2017	KOREA	KIM JONG-HEE
〃	KOREA	PARK YOUN-KI
〃	KOREA	KANG YOUNG-DUK

Year	Country	Winners
2018	KOREA	HONG YUN-PYEO
〃	KOREA	JEON HONG-GU
2019	KOREA	KIM JEONG-WON
〃	KOREA	JUNG HYUN-IM
〃	KOREA	YOON HYOUNG-SOON
2020	KOREA	PARK YOUNG-YUL
〃	KOREA	CHUN BYUNG-OK
〃	KOREA	LEE EUI-YOUNG
2021	KOREA	CHOI SUN-AE
〃	KOREA	LEE GYU-IK
〃	KOREA	LIM BYEONG-JEON
2022	KOREA	BAE YOUNG-SUK
〃	KOREA	JU JUNG-HYUN
2023	KOREA	KOO MYONG-SOOK
〃	KOREA	KIM YOUNG-SUN
〃	KOREA	HAN TAEK-KYU
2024	KOREA	SEO KEUN-HEE
〃	GERMANY	JHUNG ANJA
〃	KOREA	YOON JEONG-IN

세계시문학회 연혁 History of the Society of the World Poetry

- 1982. 11. 26   세계시문학회 창립총회 초대 김영삼 회장 취임
- 1982~1993   정기총회(매년 상반기)

- 1994. 6. 27   세계시문학회 제2대 김정웅 회장 취임
- 1994~2012   정기총회(매년 상반기)

- 1998. 12. 5   제16집 세계시문학 출판기념회 및 제12회 세계시 가야금관왕관상 시상식
- 1999. 11. 27   제17집 세계시문학 출판기념회 및 제13회 세계시 가야금관왕관상 시상식
- 2000. 11. 24   제18집 세계시문학 출판기념회 및 제14회 세계시 가야금관왕관상 시상식
- 2001. 11. 29   제19집 세계시문학 출판기념회 및 제15회 세계시 가야금관왕관상 시상식
- 2002. 11. 22   제20집 세계시문학 출판기념회 및 제16회 세계시 가야금관왕관상 시상식
- 2003. 11. 19   제21집 세계시문학 출판기념회 및 제17회 세계시 가야금관왕관상 시상식
- 2004. 11. 3   제22집 세계시문학 출판기념회 및 제18회 세계시 가야금관왕관상 시상식
- 2005. 11. 16   제23집 세계시문학 출판기념회 및 제19회 세계시 가야금관왕관상 시상식
- 2006. 11. 16   제24집 세계시문학 출판기념회 및 제20회 세계시 가야금관왕관상 시상식
- 2007. 10. 26   제25집 세계시문학 출판기념회 및 제21회 세계시 가야금관왕관상 시상식
- 2008. 11. 8   제26집 세계시문학 출판기념회 및 제22회 세계시 가야금관왕관상 시상식
- 2009. 12. 17   제27집 세계시문학 출판기념회 및 제23회 세계시 가야금관왕관상 시상식
- 2010. 11. 19   제28집 세계시문학 출판기념회 및 제24회 세계시 가야금관왕관상 시상식
- 2011. 11. 11   제29집 세계시문학 출판기념회 및 제25회 세계시 가야금관왕관상 시상식

- 2012. 6.27~30 본회 창립 30주년기념 한몽 문학교류 심포지엄 및 세계시 낭송회
- 2012. 11. 9   제30집 세계시문학 출판기념회 및 제26회 세계시 가야금관왕관상 시상식

- 2013. 7.17~18 세계시문학회 심포지엄 및 낭송회(전북 고창)
- 2013. 10. 4   세계시문학회 제3대 정송전 회장 취임
- 2013. 11. 29   제31집 세계시문학 출판기념회 및 제27회 세계시 가야금관왕관상 시상식

- 2014. 4.1~2   세계시문학회 제32차 세미나(경북 경주)
- 2014. 6. 24   세계시문학회 제4대 원응순 회장 취임

- 2014. 12. 18　　제32집 세계시문학 출판기념회 및 제28회 세계시문학상 시상식
- 2015. 11. 24　　제33집 세계시문학 출판기념회 및 제29회 세계시문학상 시상식
- 2016. 3. 31~4. 1　문학기행 및 시낭송회(전남 순천·구례 일원)
- 2016. 10. 26　　한·중 시문학 세미나 및 시화전(2016. 10. 15~11. 20)
- 2016. 11. 29　　제34집 세계시문학 출판기념회 및 제30회 세계시문학상 시상식
- 2017. 2. 21　　제36차 정기총회
- 2017. 3. 23　　확대 임원회의 및 이사 추대식
- 2017. 4. 25　　문학기행 및 시낭송회(경기도 여주 일원)
- 2017. 9. 1　　유관순시단과 함께하는 시낭송회
- 2017. 10. 14　　난빛축제와 함께하는 시낭송회
- 2017. 11. 28　　제35집 세계시문학 출판기념회 및 제31회 세계시문학상 시상식
- 2018. 2. 20　　제37차 정기총회
- 2018. 4. 27　　문학기행 (충남 당진 심훈문학관 일대)
- 2018. 6. 26　　임원회의 및 이사 추대식
- 2018. 10. 20　　난빛축제와 함께하는 시화전
- 2018. 11. 23　　제36집 세계시문학 출판기념회 및 제32회 세계시문학상 시상식
- 2019. 2. 19　　제 38차 정기총회-합정동 들풀
- 2019. 3. 26　　세계시문학회 제6대 오진환 회장 취임
　　　　　　　　회장 이 취임식 및 임원·이사 위촉식
- 2019. 4. 23　　봄 문학기행-강원도 양구, 두타연, 평화의 댐 일원
- 2019. 6. 3~7　　라오스 해외 문학 연수-동독국립대학교, 비엔티안, 방비엥 일원
- 2019. 9. 24　　시낭송회-인사동 시가연
- 2019. 10. 24　　가을 문학기행-충북 소월·경암 문학기념관 방문 후
　　　　　　　　수안보파크호텔 알프스홀에서 문학특강 및 시낭송회
- 2019. 11. 7　　임원회의-합정동 들풀
- 2019. 11. 27　　제37집 세계시문학 출판기념회 및 제33회 세계시문학상 시상식

- 2020. 5. 26　　임원회의-합정동 들풀
- 2020. 6. 4　　제39차 정기총회-합정동 들풀
- 2020. 10. 13　　문학기행-윤동주문학관 탐방
- 2020. 10. 27　　문학특강 및 시낭송회-인사동 시가연
- 2020. 11. 26　　제38집 세계시문학 출판기념회 및 제34회 세계시문학상 시상식

- 2021. 2. 24　　임원회의-합정동 들풀
- 2021. 5. 12　　제40차 정기총회-토정로 영풍상가
　　　　　　　　세계시문학회 제7대 박영률 회장 취임
- 2021. 12. 15　　제39집 세계시문학 출판기념회 및 제35회 세계시문학상 시상식

- 2022. 5. 9　　임원회의-토정로 영풍상가
- 2022. 5. 24　　제41차 정기총회-합정동 들풀
- 2022. 6. 16　　봄 문학기행-강원도 원주 박경리뮤지엄 일원
- 2022. 7. 5　　문학특강 및 시낭송회-인사동 시가연
- 2022. 10. 25　　가을 문화 탐방-서울 미당 서정주의 집 일원
- 2022. 11. 30　　제40집 세계시문학 출판기념회 및 제36회 세계시문학상 시상식

- 2023. 5. 2　　임원회의-합정동 들풀
- 2023. 5. 18　　제42차 정기총회-합정동 들풀
　　　　　　　　제42차 정기총회-회장 재추대. 임원·감사 연임
- 2023. 6. 1　　문화 탐방 및 시낭송회 - 문학의집·서울
- 2023. 8. 28~9. 1　해외 문학기행(백두산 서파, 대련, 고구려 유적지 일원)
- 2023. 12. 20　　제41집 세계시문학 출판기념회 및 제37회 세계시문학상 시상식

- 2024. 2. 29　　제43차 정기총회-합정동 들풀
- 2024. 5. 30　　봄 문학기행-강원도 영월(청령포, 장릉, 김삿갓유적지 일원)
- 2024. 8. 28　　임원회의-합정동 투썸
- 2024. 10. 15　　임원회의-합정동 다북어국
- 2024. 10. 17　　가을 문학기행-충북 충주 수안보파크호텔 알프스홀에서 문학특강
- 2024. 12. 11　　제42집 세계시문학 출판기념회 및 제38회 세계시문학상 시상식

세계시문학회 조직
The System of the Society of the World Poetry

- 명예회장 : 오진환
- 회　장 : 박영률
- 부회장 : 신동명 진상순 홍춘표
　　　　 박윤기 남창희 구명숙
　　　　 정지홍
- 사무총장 : 윤수아
- 사무국장 : 천병옥
- 사무차장 : 배병군
- 편집주간 : 김효열
- 편집국장 : 김돈영
- 기획국장 : 윤윤근
- 국제외교국장 : 김의식
- 해외국장 : 박인애
- 운영국장 : 주정현
- 홍보국장 : 서근희
- 총무국장 : 고방규
- 감사 : 이규익 형정희

- 고 문 : 김종상 엄기원 유승우
　　　　 김봉군 손해일 권오운
　　　　 정송전 원응순

- 자문위원 : 김남웅　서정남
　　　　　 이상진

- 이 사 : 이창수 홍윤표 장동석
　　　　 방정순 최순애 배영숙
　　　　 이병석 안금식 연기영
　　　　 정숙자 이의영 한정원
　　　　 오숙현 윤　자 김민경
　　　　 이풍호 윤정인

(무순)

세계시문학 제42집(2024)

인쇄 2024년 12월 5일
발행 2024년 12월 11일

발행인　박영률
편집주간　김효열
편집위원　신동명 윤수아 박윤기 남창희 정지홍
　　　　　구명숙 김돈영 천병옥 배병군

발행처　**세계시문학회**
주소　　서울시 마포구 양화진길41, 일신오피스텔 603호
전자우편　wp1982@hanmail.net
우편번호　04083

제작처　**을지출판공사**
전화　　02-334-4050　　팩시밀리 02-334-4010

값 30,000원

ISBN 978-89-7566-243 0　　　03810

세계시문학회 계좌번호
농협 301-0246-6480-91 세계시문학회(오진환)